Neeraj Kapoor has spent nearly three decades in the industry; the first eighteen as a corporate professional and the last eleven as an entrepreneur. He is a transformational leader, who has helped thousands of people see unprecedented breakthroughs in their life and career. He is the founder of Start-up Business Academy, a global initiative to empower entrepreneurs to launch and rapidly scale up their businesses with proven systems.

As one of India's greatest brand builders, recognized on the global stage, Neeraj is on a mission to enable aspiring entrepreneurs to turn their business dreams into profitable global brands with ease, grace, power and simplicity.

This book aims to offer world-class, practical, step-by-step guidance, focused on spiritual, mental, physical and emotional mastery towards unlocking the exceptional value of your talent, transcending new paradigms, exploring new opportunities and rewriting your own destiny.

FROM STUCK-UP TO START-UP

A PRACTICAL GUIDE TO STARTING YOUR OWN VENTURE

NEERAJ KAPOOR

BUSINESS

An imprint of Penguin Random House

PENGUIN BUSINESS

USA | Canada | UK | Ireland | Australia
New Zealand | India | South Africa | China

Penguin Business is part of the Penguin Random House group of companies
whose addresses can be found at global.penguinrandomhouse.com

Published by Penguin Random House India Pvt. Ltd
4th Floor, Capital Tower 1, MG Road,
Gurugram 122 002, Haryana, India

Penguin
Random House
India

First published in Penguin Business by Penguin Random House India 2022

ISBN 9780143457138

Typeset in Adobe Garamond Pro by MAP Systems, Bangalore, India
Printed at Thomson Press India Ltd, New Delhi

www.penguin.co.in

This book is dedicated to the HERO IN YOU

ॐ अज्ञानतिमिरान्धस्य ज्ञानाञ्जनशालाकया।
चक्षुरुन्मीलितं येन तस्मै श्रीगुरवे नमः॥

I was born in the darkest of ignorance.
My guru opened my eyes with the torch of knowledge.
I offer my respectful obeisance unto him.

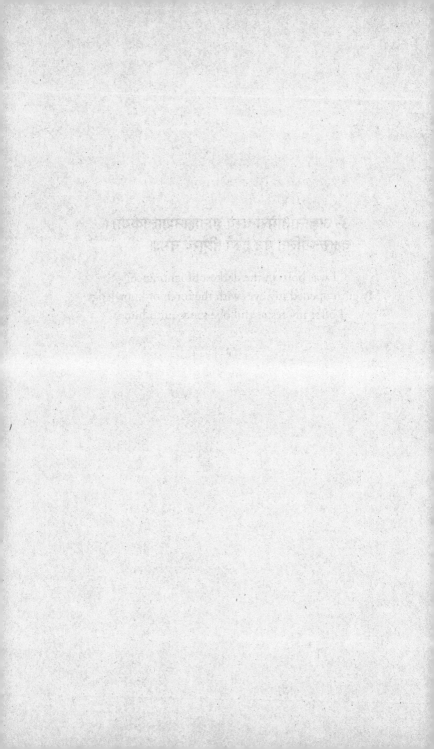

Contents

Part 1
Honey-Trapped

Part 2
Discovery

Part 3
Action

Author's Note

If you have a dream in your heart and fire in your belly, then this book will empower you to launch a start-up *even without quitting your (cosy or not-so-cosy) job*.

Feel free to read this book right through on a fast track. However, if you would like to slowly go through the concepts in *From Stuck-Up to Start-Up*, I invite you to visit https://app.startupsecrets.in/ to receive a weekly video that will coincide with your learning each week for the next seventy days. In less than three months from now, you will have a business education that most business schools don't teach in their most expensive courses charging lakhs of rupees. This book is designed to transform you from being a stuck-up employee to a start-up entrepreneur who has the practical mindset and the skill set to move from where you are to where you want to be.

To receive the weekly videos that accompany the wisdom of this book, visit https://app.startupsecrets.in/

To get the most from this book:

1. Read the book at a scheduled time, daily at least for thirty to forty-five minutes.
2. Watch one video per week for the next ten weeks.
3. Complete the exercises given in the book diligently with 100 per cent integrity.

4. Practise the learnings from the book in your daily life to
   emerge as a successful start-up entrepreneur.

https://app.startupsecrets.in/

Introduction

Welcome.
Are you ready for your dream
start-up to show up?

Whether you are a professional or a seasoned entrepreneur, one thing is for sure: the book you are holding in your hand will take your experience to another level.

That's because the book you are about to read is unlike any other book that has been written before. Nothing can fully replace your own experiences that transform your life—but I have been obsessed with finding a solution to enable you to experience and deliver transformative breakthroughs right from the comfort of your chair.

This is not just a book. You are about to experience what happens when you combine the power of words plus my personal mission to enable 50 million people to break through and transform their dream start-up into reality with ease and grace. To get the most out of investing your time in this book, I have put together a collection of items that will serve you during your experience. I hope you enjoy these gifts and use them throughout your journey to accelerate your transformation.

These are located at the end of each chapter under the 'Free Resources' section.

As you start your journey, take note:

'You are way more powerful than what you believe about yourself. Once you experience the real you, you shall have the power to transform your grandest vision and biggest dreams to manifest into a reality, with ease and grace.'

This book is a step towards enabling you to make your dreams, vision and desires a reality that can change the world, your world to begin with. Make sure you are ready to receive this gift of life with open arms.

April 2022   Neeraj Kapoor
                                              Mumbai, India

Prologue

When the idea of writing a book that would show the way to those aspiring to become entrepreneurs took root, I spent a few hours jotting down the thoughts fluttering in my mind. At that point, all I could think of was my own story of how I broke the job trap and became an entrepreneur. From being a person who had lived on fat salary packages in the cosy shell of job security and with India's greatest brand builder award, what was the turn of some events which took away the ground from under my feet? At that point, I could have taken a decision to find another cocoon to survive in or taken a plunge into a different orbit that was risky but also promising to my heart, which desired freedom. I took the second path, 'the road less travelled', which M. Scott Peck talks about in his book.

But the real reason for me to choose entrepreneurship as my path was not really the desire to have something of my own. I did desire freedom but not from my work. I desired freedom so I could be with my family whenever I wanted. Most often, business is seen as a rational process that moves you away from your family, but I never thought that my family could be the reason I would pursue my business. Never before could I have imagined that entrepreneurship would bring me closer to my family than ever before.

The illusion of security that I was living in earlier was broken, in not a very pleasing way, but I thank my dad who in heaven guided me to take the new path. It was risky and full of bumps, but I did survive at the start and later thrived. Over the time of my discoveries as an entrepreneur, I also saw others breaking the status quo and launching themselves into the pool of entrepreneurial freedom. Unfortunately, I saw most aspiring entrepreneurs were unable to break the trap of job security. And some also failed in their effort within a few years.

As I researched more about what kept great minds from taking the plunge, and what made creative risk-takers fail in their attempts, I was astounded to find that a vast majority of humanity goes to their graves with their talent undiscovered. It's like throwing away an expensive birthday gift without even opening the wrapping paper. It was clear to me that there is only a very little percentage that ventures out in the open and dares to start something of their own and write their own destiny. Most just succumb to modern-day slavery.

And, this was not all, I was further intrigued by some startling statistics that over 70 per cent of all new start-ups shut down in the first three years and 70 per cent of the rest in the next three to five years.

Who am I? Why am I here? Why do a few people live a grand life of abundance while most others toil away in the world of meagre survival? Is this all destined? I could see that I, along with many others, was trapped in the world of survival and I had no way to get out of that. Can I break through this lifestyle? How can I break through?

These questions formed the fundamental queries when I sat down to find out the answers, but there were no answers coming from tonnes of research and hours, days and weeks of going through the various literature. Finally, after months of soul-searching, in one of the meditation sessions, I started to get clarity. The answers were coming to me. Immediately, I started to jot down the points, and as if I had opened up a powerful hose, the answers started to flow to me with utmost clarity.

That is what the foundation of this book became. As you dive into this book, you will see through the pain that is holding you back and, at the same time, it will also give you the courage to move up. The cage that you might currently be in can easily be broken—this is what I want to share with you. But I would not push you out into the hard world without the right tools for fighting. Instead, I will give you a way to build a foundation first and prepare yourself in a way that you can ensure your success after you take your first step.

I would consider it my contribution to your life and to society, if, after reading this book, you are able to take the first bold step in the direction of your dreams, or you are able to pull yourself out of the crazy loop of fighting for survival into the world of abundance. The moment would be most gratifying for me, when you succeed in launching your start-up without quitting your job, unlock the exponential value of your talent, transcend new paradigms (explore new opportunities), write your own destiny and start creating a legacy for your next generation.

Part 1: Honey-Trapped

Time to See Where You Are
Assess Your Situation

Chapter 1

A Train of Thoughts

When life turned upside down for me in one day

It was a bright, sunny morning, just like any other day. I had no clue that this day was going to change my entire life forever. One single day has so many moments to live, during the course of which things can make, break and topple your life. On that one day, you can take a deep plunge on a rollercoaster ride, leaving its trail behind for you to cherish and get ready to move on to a different paradigm.

How It Happened

I was busy with morning chores and was prepping for another usual day at the office when my phone rang.

'Congrats.' It was my elder brother on the phone.

'Thanks, *bhaiya*,' I replied, having no clue as to why he was congratulating me.

'Didn't you check the morning ET [*Economic Times* newspaper]?' he asked. 'You have been featured as one of India's greatest brand builders,' he said with excitement in his voice.

His words were like a camera flash on my face, and I was suddenly speechless. I imagined myself walking proudly on a wide stage, waving to a large, boisterous crowd cheering me.

I thanked him and sought his blessings. In that fleeting moment of exuberance, I rushed to pick up the newspaper from my table. And when I saw my bright smiling face printed there and read the wonderful words that described my achievements, I felt proud and tall. Immersed in my happy thoughts, I quickly got ready. I couldn't wait to see the response on the faces of people who worked in my office. I drove to the office with a broad smile and true delight on my face.

As the chief marketing officer for i-mint, India's largest loyalty programme, I was doing extremely well, or so I thought. It was the day our company's prospective investor's verdict was to be announced. It was an important day I was looking forward to.

I parked and walked straight to the office. Everything looked bright and sunny to me. The office peon waved me a good morning and served me fresh coconut water. The coconut water that usually tasted bland pleased my palate! As I reached my cabin carrying the cup, the intercom rang. Anjali, the receptionist, greeted me with her particularly warm voice.

'Good morning, sir,' she said, adding, 'the boss is in the conference room waiting for you.'

I thanked her and quickly gulped down some coconut nectar, picked up my task diary and a folder from my desk, and headed towards my boss's cabin. On my way there, I saw a few colleagues smiling at me and, as they came to congratulate me on my achievement, I responded with a blissful beam on my face.

This hearty welcome was expected but not the strange look on a few faces from those who seemed to be not in their true element. For a brief moment, I wondered what was going on. As I entered the meeting room, I felt a knot in the pit of my stomach. I expected that the boss had called to congratulate me on my amazing feat, but my intuitive mind was telling me that something was not right. I wondered, what could possibly be the update the CEO wanted to discuss? Did we not get a sign-up from the investor? Did we not get the right valuation? Did the meeting not happen? My head was soon filled with questions.

Still flipping through the predictions in my head, I knocked on the door and Vijay, my CEO, welcomed me with a warm handshake, 'Hey Neeraj,' he said in a typical Silicon Valley accent, 'how have you been?'

'Good morning, Vijay,' I replied, 'I am awesome. And how was your meeting with the investors?' I asked.

'Superb,' he said with a twinkle in his eyes as we both sat down.

I felt relaxed. My worries seemed to have been unfounded. I was glad to know that the status was positive, took a deep breath and said, 'That's nice,' while looking to dig deeper for more details.

'Well,' the boss continued, 'I have good news to share with you because you have been the top performer and you deserve to hear it first.'

'Oh, I am glad you are sharing it with me,' I said and added with a smile, 'what's the good news, Vijay, I am all ears!'

'Neeraj, after months of labour, finally we have an investor on board, we signed the shareholder agreement last night and have got some amazing valuations. 10X, to be precise, in a matter of three years,' he said.

'That's great, Vijay,' but my sixth sense told me that something was not right. 'So, what's the catch?' I asked him upfront, looking straight into his eyes.

Unprepared for the straight question, he paused, his voice fluttered, but then he spilled the beans, 'Well, the investor is picking up 85 per cent of the equity, and if all goes well, they would soon like to have their own management team and would like to do things their own way. You can expect many changes.'

He paused briefly, and before I could absorb it, he continued, 'You would be reporting to an expat and can expect certain restructuring in your role and responsibilities.'

The declaration was made subtly, but it did not change the fact that we were now having a new set of bosses to report to, a new management. I maintained a stoic silence for a very brief time in which I continued looking at him with my inquisitively speculative eyes. My mind was running on overdrive, but my mouth was not letting out a word.

'You mean, you have sold the company to a foreign player for the money,' I could not hold my feeling of shock for long. 'That's like selling your most prized possession.' I first expressed my disappointment calmly, but after a brief pause, my mind almost blasted him, 'Do you even realize the pains that we have taken to raise this baby from nothing to what it is today? Would you do that to your children?'

When my mind calmed down, I finally heard him, '. . . they plan to come in with their own thoughts on how to make things work. So, gear up to team up with them. And just to be practical, see if you have options open in the marketplace for your role will be curtailed. There may be fewer privileges, authority. Roles and responsibility will be trimmed . . .' In words that were not said, he was saying, 'Buddy, look for another job. I would if I were you! It's all part of the game. Best of luck!'

The gravity of the situation did not hit me at that moment, but only later did I realize that this was serious. Our next 'huddle-up' team meeting, which was normally conducted to review performances and where the heads of the organization delivered motivational talks, had a different agenda this time. It was the day of celebration and the news of the change was afloat. As the head of my team, I was supposed to share this so-called good news with the team, which I did. But inside I felt compassion for the naive team that was delighted, unaware of what was in store for them, something I could not tell them. They were expecting positive changes and nothing drastic, but what was really going to happen was discovered only later. I was experiencing my share of disappointment in silence, but I was not going to be there to see theirs.

From a Train of Thoughts to a Realization

The announcement was no newsflash, but it was to change my life. What I deciphered was a clear and bold statement: 'Well, Mr Kapoor, you have done a wonderful job, helped us increase the valuation of the company from Rs 20 crore to around Rs 200 crore, and now, your efforts got us an investor on board. All we needed from you has been accomplished. So, we don't need your services any more! You have a choice to move on . . .'

As I sat at my desk, my heart sank and my hands turned icy-cold with the AC vent blowing right on me. What would I do? What would I tell my team? How would I face my family? What if my team members were laid off? I felt like a failure and an awarded loser. That reminded me of the story of one Mohandas Gandhi who was once thrown out of a train in South Africa despite having a valid ticket just because he was in a foreign land. Now, I felt the same. This was not my land. It never belonged to me, no matter how hard I worked for it.

Even on my drive back home, the questions kept rebounding in my head: What is my life for? What am I doing? What's next? What is going on? How are companies behaving? How are employers treating their employees? Is my boss fair? Are they abusing or exploiting . . . what are they doing?

I looked at the 'Y' fork ahead in the road and I felt like it was the crossroads of my life. While on the physical road, I knew which turn to take; in my life, I was clueless and unsure.

My mind jumped to childhood memories of my father. He had once shared insights full of wisdom while taking an evening stroll with me in a nearby park, 'Every situation has two perspectives, one that is empowering, and the other disempowering. You always have a choice. Remember, beta, first you *make* choices, then *choices make you*.' A simple but powerful truth and I was ready to decide on my choice.

'Thank you, Papa, for showing me the way,' I murmured, looking up to the heavens. I had lost my dad while I was busy with my ambitious career, and had lost a chance to be with him when he breathed his last. In that moment, it started becoming clear to me that I had lost a lot in pursuing my career dreams. Whatever happened on that day, I was not prepared for, nor was I prepared for what had dawned on me a few years back.

Unprepared for the Loss

Back in 2003, I was in Pune busy climbing the corporate ladder. I found an opportunity to work with the billionaire Firodia family and the brand Kinetic (remember the famous Kinetic Honda). Two new models, Kinetic Nova and Zing, were going to be launched. Both were targeted at upwardly mobile urban consumers with a passion for style and personality. For that target group, purchasing decisions would not come easily, so we had to work very hard on marketing. I was handling the marketing campaign for the launch, and during that time, I was travelling with Bollywood stars like Suniel Shetty and Karisma Kapoor for the launch events in over ten cities across the country. It was a super busy time, and the Kinetic marketing campaign was an important project of my life.

My parents were in Agra at that time. My father had retired from the defence services and was getting old and weak. He was at an age when he needed his son by his side. Unfortunately, I was busy executing my project plans. For his well-being, I was relying on my sister who would keep me updated with Dad's health status every now and then. The marketing campaign was going to be over soon, and I had already planned a visit to see my dad. So, I worked hard and was eager to do a good job so I could meet him and tell him my heroic stories that I knew he would love to hear.

Unfortunately, the launch project got extended and I had to postpone my trip home. While I was making arrangements for the trip at a later date, my dad called and asked, 'Are you coming tomorrow, beta?' With a heavy heart, I replied, 'I am sorry, Dad. I have to postpone my trip but I am going to be there soon.'

I had no idea what the next morning was going to bring me. Early, while it was still a little dark, I woke up startled by my mobile ringing. I looked at the bedside table where my phone's screen was flickering with an image of my mother. My mom is an early riser, but she would never call me at that hour unless it was urgent. I answered her call immediately.

Before I could even say hello, I heard her say in a sombre tone, 'Dad is going, beta.' My heart skipped a beat, and in the next silent second, I could sense the lump in her throat. I was sitting thousands of kilometres away and could do nothing at that moment except promise my mother that I would be home as soon as it was possible.

'I know I am late but I will . . .' Before I could finish my promise, she said, 'Beta, you are not late. You are too late.' The helplessness in her voice was apparent, and it was mirrored in my voice too. The sun was now visible on the eastern horizon, but all I felt was gloomy darkness floating around me. While mornings normally brought freshness, that day, it brought incessant tears to my heart; a few of them started to roll down my cheeks.

I was working on a big project so I could chase big money, but I thought about what I was losing to pursue it and that I was going to pay a heavy price, a very heavy price. In that moment of truth, when I knew that I would lose my dad, and that no matter how much money I had, I might never get a chance to even see him, I felt like I was back to zero. All that money and pride in work was for nothing. I felt like bursting into tears but I did not have time for even that. I could not lose hope yet. I wiped my tears and rushed to get ready. The next few moments were hazy, and while I was getting ready for the airport, I had only one prayer continuously going on in my head. I wished I could get there on time to see my father alive.

Every second of my journey was restless that day—from home to Mumbai airport, I drove like crazy that morning, covering the distance in one hour, thirty-five minutes, from plane to taxi, and then a six-hour-drive to my dad. It took me twelve hours, and in those twelve dreadful hours, I kept praying to God, wishing my dad would live for some more time. When I reached my house, I saw a crowd lined up, dressed in white clothes. White—the colour of death—and in that moment, I knew that I was indeed too late and had lost the last chance to see my dad alive. None of my prayers were answered and why would they be? God had given me a chance earlier. I could have got there on time, but I did not because I had to take care of my responsibilities at work. I could no longer hold my tears back and it was as if a dam had burst.

My dad was my responsibility too. He was my love, my inspiration, my friend, my strength, my buddy—and for my job, I lost all, lost the chance to bid him a last goodbye. I did not even know if he was in pain or found peace while leaving this earth.

I slowly walked to my dad with heavy steps. I could feel him, the body was still warm, but I knew that he was gone. I could see him, his satisfied, peaceful face, his half-open eyes as if those were still waiting for me, but he would not talk to me. The truth hit me with a thud—I had lost my dad, I was never going to see him again, and I had also lost the chance to speak to him on the last day of his life. And not just that, I could also not fulfil his last wish of having his son close to him. Everyone was there except his own son. All that was left for me to do was give him the last wave and see his body vanishing in flames at the cremation ground alongside the River Yamuna.

As the sun was setting over the western horizon, far in the background I could see the famous Taj Mahal—the symbol of love and sacrifice, a place where my father first took me years ago.

I could have come earlier. My boss had not stopped me. And yet, I felt I did not have the luxury to come sooner because I had trapped myself in a job and burdened myself with work responsibilities. I felt like someone had put tonnes of stones on my chest and I could not move. I was unprepared for that moment. I was unprepared for the loss of my father. And the burden of guilt was so huge that I could not take it. I also knew that I had to live with it for the rest of my life, and that was killing me.

I used to take pride in managing big projects as if I was the king of the jungle. I thought I was a lion but I was actually a trapped lion who was trained every day to obey and only obey, with no freedom to live its own life. The flashbacks of my life upset me. It was 2003 when I lost my dad for my job, and several years later, I was losing my job; but for what?

That day taught me a lot. In an instant, I had the realization that all those years I had been working not for myself but for my employers so they could run their show and make wealth. I had no direction, purpose, or plan of my own. I was leading my life according to somebody else's plan. And I was not going to do it any more. I was not ready to lose more in life. I wanted to look for other options.

In life and in business, either you have a plan for yourself, or someone has a plan for you. Choose wisely!

What Were My Options?

Look for another job till the time the investor came on board or do something that I had always wanted to do—launch my own start-up.

I could see that one road would lead me to my dream with unlimited possibilities of breakthroughs in life, and the other would throw me into the same old grind. One route was the road less travelled—the one with excitement and that I had no experience of in life. The traditional road was more familiar, safer and appreciated by everyone. The exciting road had uncertainties spread across and was like an adventure in an unknown jungle.

Despite the fact that the idea of entrepreneurship appealed to me, I was filled with doubts. *The Road Less Travelled*, the title of the book by M. Scott Peck, buzzed in my head and I asked myself: 'Where would it lead me to?'

I had no experience as an entrepreneur. I did not know how to justify my action if I took such a path. The big question that stared at me was: Should I try? But if I did not try and kept on doing the same thing that I was doing till then, I was going to live the same life and face the same challenges as I was facing. I recalled the words of the American TV presenter Steve Harvey, 'If you keep doing what you have been doing, you will keep getting what you have been getting.'

If I continued on the same path, I would still be trapped. I would still not have time for my family and myself. I really wanted to do something about it. I had lost enough, and I was not going to lose more.

However, I was still not sure because leaving the safer path was a big risk. I thought that there was no harm in considering the possibility and finding out what it had to offer. So, I reached out to a dear friend who was already an entrepreneur. He was excited to hear my voice when I called. We were connecting after a long time, and we immediately decided to meet for lunch.

On a chilly winter day, under a mild sun, I relished hot soup with my old friend and was excited to hear what he had to say. We began by sharing stories of our lives, and soon started to compare our careers.

He said with pride in his voice, 'Sir, I am a year younger than you, but I haven't ever taken up a job. I have always been into business. You know your net worth; what do you think is my net worth?'

After doing some rough calculations in my head, I threw out a number, 'Rs 20 crore.'

My friend smiled and replied modestly, 'Add another zero to that, sir.'

My eyes popped out and I said, 'What? Oh my god! You mean Rs 200 crore! Are you seriously that rich? Or are you simply pepping me up?'

One extra zero, and the sun started to shine brighter. The path was precarious, but it did come with a possibility of making it big, really big! Without losing any more precious moments, I thought how easy it was for my friend to say yes to our meeting. I was never so privileged in my job. I could not say yes to a friend for a meeting without looking at my calendar, because my calendar was not decided by me but by my company. Here, my friend was sitting in front of me with a net worth much more than mine, and I was busier with less net worth.

'Yes, sir. I am telling you the truth, and this is the result of my walking on an absolutely different path,' he said, with confidence and a bright smile that I rarely saw on people working in my office.

After this interaction, I was so moved that I gathered up the courage to share my dilemma with him. I told him about the takeover and the job scene at my office. I also told him that I was having second thoughts about taking up a job and wanted to explore the possibilities of rowing my own boat.

He said, 'You must choose entrepreneurship. And the reasons are: first, age is in your favour, and second, the corporate world is always open to grab you in case you don't succeed with your venture. So why not try? After all, you have been in the industry for some time, proven yourself and to top it all, have got awarded as India's greatest brand builder.'

It felt as though I had already made up my mind to do what he was suggesting but was waiting for a little push or perhaps some assurance from someone who had done it. I knew that I had a choice—either take the road that I had taken all my life, or choose to venture into uncharted territory.

The decision was not easy. It never is because, even if your heart pushes you forward and you want to believe that you can do it, there is a lot at stake and you know that your new path may not be easy. I was in a dilemma. I had decided but my decision was half-cooked until I met my friend, who became a catalyst, pushing me in the right direction. And yet, I was nervous and in two minds.

My head was flipping a coin. On the one side of it were the flashes of my past that disappointed me, where I disappointed my family, and they were adding fuel to my fire to launch the new drive. The other side was pumped by my rational self that was stopping me. I asked myself again and again why I was unable to take a decision and I was also having doubts about whether I would stick to my plan. I was also facing the fear of failure. But even if I failed, I could always go back to my old life; this was the only justification that logically fitted in my head.

While I was so keen on finding a logical justification to give in to the idea of entrepreneurship, I should have known that our decisions are always emotional and only later do we search for the logic to justify our actions. Psychological studies have revealed that the heart is the primary lever behind all our decisions. So, I sensed that the only thing that was stopping me was the fear of the unknown. For a moment, I thought, if only I did not fear failure but believed that I could do it, I would not take so long to dive in.

One Last Push

On the way back home, after my brief rendezvous with my friend, I kept thinking. I repeated to myself, 'In life, it's not the capability that you have, but the choices that you make that determine your destiny.' My head was still evaluating the two sides of the coin, trying to take a final decision that would allow me to put my feet firmly on one side.

While driving through a posh lane, I spotted a few stray dogs. I was living in a suburb of Mumbai, the megacity and business capital of India. This busy city had uncountable vehicles crossing streets every day and in almost every corner of the city, you would often see these dogs chasing cars. They would bark, run in packs and usually disturb our peace. They would keep following cars as if trying to catch them, but their fanciful aggression would end after a while when they would stop, bark some more, turn around and stare at each other, as if saying, 'I think we did a good job.' And then, they would go back to their routine.

This sequence would be repeated numerous times a day for almost all vehicles. Their actions bore no purpose. They wanted no food. They had no love for cars. And yet, there was amusement in the mere act. While I could easily ignore them, I could not ignore the humans standing on the sides of the roads who were not any less restless than the dogs.

People waiting for trains at stations and buses at stands would also chase vehicles, except with a purpose to get inside one that would take them to their destination. At times, in Mumbai locals, a few of them could be found hanging on the edge and risking their lives every day. Some even die as they cross the tracks in a rush and are run over by trains. These same people are forced to live in cramped compartment-like homes where they struggle to even stretch their legs while sleeping. Most of their lives are lived in compartments. As I moved my car to the highway, I took a careful look at the worn-out and worried human faces. I wondered: Is this the kind of life they dreamt of when they were younger?

Do they even know what they are doing and why they are doing it?

If I could ask them why they were running like mad dogs, they would possibly give the following reasons:

- Oh, I am travelling to work, and it's part of my daily routine.
- I work for a living.

- I have to pay my bills.
- I work to pay off my loans and credit card bills.
- I have a family to take care of.

Most of these people, living so uneventfully, looked well-educated, but I wondered if this was the life they had imagined when they were spending huge amounts on their studies.

This is how people in jobs live, not just in Mumbai but in most big cities around the world. Some visuals of trains in Tokyo or London have even gone viral on social media with videos showing people pushed into compartments like animals, so that the doors could be closed. We laugh at these jokes but are their lives also a joke?

The commotion on the road looked like nothing less than one big mirage that everyone was chasing. Then how are we different from dogs? Even worse, we are actually working like donkeys, except that the bags on our backs don't carry sugar or rice but something more sophisticated like a laptop. And it is not crazy but acceptable, for there is a rat race that you cannot afford to lose, so you keep running to not be left behind.

How do you feel when you receive an SMS at the end of the month which says: 'Dear customer, your account xxxxxxxxx has been credited with INR 5xxxxx.00. Info: Salary,' That is what we all wait for and that was what I was also doing every month, month on month, for years. Rat, dog, donkey or lion—what was I? I would prefer to be called a lion, albeit a tame one, or the one who could be called the king of his own life!

I realized that if I had to take a firm decision, I needed strength and high self-esteem. So, I said to myself, looking into the rear-view mirror of the car, 'Neeraj, You have all the ingredients for making it in business. If worse comes to worst, even if you don't make it big, your age is on your side. You can always come back to take up a job.' That made me feel mentally stronger and clearer.

I had spent eighteen years as a corporate slave, and missed important events of my life, including the birth of my son and the last day in my father's life. I wasn't there for my family most of the time. I was running like a madman chasing one transaction after the other for the company I worked for, thinking that I was a loyal commander winning battles one after the other for my leaders. Little did I realize that I was a mere pawn in the circus who was following the orders of a ringmaster. I realized that in the corporate race, even if you are a powerful lion walking proudly, you are still trapped and tamed by a ringmaster.

I decided to do something on my own because I wanted to be a lion but not a tame one. Society does not need more tame lions but leaders who live according to their choice. And if I could be the biggest brand builder for companies I worked for, then why not for myself? When I worked for big companies, I had a belief in me that I could manage any kind of complexity and make any brand grow. I reminded myself of this and asked myself to hold on to this faith I had in myself as I took the next steps.

Key Takeaways

- You always have choices in life, and it is your selection that defines your life.
- If you only understand the purpose of your life, you will be able to make the right choice.
- If you have a dream, you will also recognize the clues that will give you reasons to pursue the dream to fruition.

- Just as you will experience positive pushes, you will also find many reasons holding you back from taking a bold step.
- Being in a job that you do not enjoy or own is like living trapped in a cage from which no one else but you can free yourself.
- In the corporate rat race, even if you win, you are still a rat!

Free Resources

https://app.startupsecrets.in/ch1

Chapter 2

How Did the Lion Get Trapped?

Once upon a time, there was a huge lion, so fierce that it could tear apart an animal from limb to limb with its jaws in no time. All the animals in the jungle were scared of the lion. One day, a fox was chasing a deer but before it could catch it, the lion proudly came in and dashed across, overtaking the fox in the game, and took the deer captive. It bit into the deer's throat and consumed the poor animal after it surrendered.

The lion looked at the fox while enjoying the meal. It saw fear and helplessness on the fox's face. It was amusing as it reminded the lion of the power it had that no one could question. The fox was annoyed but then continued its search for food elsewhere.

After that day, it became a fun game for the lion, who would prey on other animals, who were easy targets, and command its dominion, leaving the poor animals famished.

One day, the clever fox decided to teach the lion a lesson. With the help of a friend, an energetic horse, the fox spread the word about a huge lion in the nearby village where some poachers lived. Soon enough, two poachers headed to the jungle. They laid a trap for the lion by tying a deer to a tree as bait. When the proud lion saw the easy prey, it quickly came to seize the opportunity. As it came near the deer, the poachers pulled the strings, trapping the lion in the net.

The poachers sold the lion to a circus company and the fierce lion was brought to the ringmaster who was to tame the big cat. At first, the lion did not cooperate. The ringmaster did not give it food. The lion was directed to follow his commands and only then would it get food. For days, the lion went hungry, and when it could no longer hold out, it started following the orders of the ringmaster to get food in exchange.

Soon, this became a habit for the lion. Every time the lion would dance on the cue of the ringmaster, it would get some food as a reward. For the lion, getting food now became very easy as it did not have to work as hard as it used to earlier when its prey had to be chased in the jungle. All it had to do was follow the orders of the ringmaster. For months, the lion kept following the orders although it was bored by the monotony of the work.

One day, it saw a deer grazing near the circus. It looked at the animal and felt like going after it. But then, it saw the ringmaster standing on the other side with a piece of meat in his hand. It looked at the food, which reminded it of the comfort and ease it had in the circus.

'Why should I run after the deer when I have a ready piece of meat that I can take just by jumping in the circus?' it wondered. The ringmaster smiled for he now knew that the lion was truly trapped and did not need chains any more to keep it inside the circus.

Despite the lion being the most powerful creature before whom no man stood a chance, the lion did not escape from the circus. This may sound like pure foolishness and yet, it is a universal phenomenon observed in many animals. Let us take an example of an elephant. Do you know how elephants are trapped?

When the elephant is a calf, it is weak. So, elephant catchers trap it, put a small chain around its leg and tie the baby elephant to a big tree. It tries to get away and break the chain but despite many desperate trials, it never succeeds for the chain is stronger. One day, it gives up and accepts the fact that the chain is impossible to break, and it has to live a life in captivity. Time passes and the baby grows up. Now it is big and strong, and tied with a tiny rope, but it does not try to break free because the programming of its mind is already done. The big elephant is physically strong enough to break the chain with a single pull, but it would never try to, because in its mind it still believes that it cannot break the chain.

In psychology, we call this 'classical conditioning'. According to the famous psychologist Jean Piaget, classical conditioning is a type of subconscious learning that creates an automatic behavioural response to a specific stimulus because of the conditions that are regularly created. A subject would respond to the stimulus in a particular manner expecting a specific reward or outcome as a result. In the case of the lion, food was the expected reward, and to get it, the lion followed the orders of the ringmaster.

This phenomenon is not just seen in animals but also in human babies. Piaget once did an experiment on a baby: A baby was put in a playroom where there were lots of toys. The baby was attracted to a soft toy, a white rabbit, and loved to play with it.

He picked up the rabbit and caressed it gently as if it was his baby. For a while, the boy kept playing with his new friend. After some time, the little baby heard a loud bang. He got scared and threw the toy on the ground. The sound stopped after a while and the baby was fine. He picked up the toy again, but this time, the instant the toy was picked up, the same loud bang was repeated. The baby threw the rabbit away again. This was repeated several times.

Every time the baby picked up the rabbit, there was a bang. After some time, the baby started associating the fear produced by the sound of the bang with the toy and started fearing the toy instead of just the sound. After a while, even when no sound was produced, the baby would start crying the moment it saw the rabbit. The baby was conditioned to fear the white rabbit.

Just like the elephant and the baby—who was conditioned to not play with the harmless white rabbit—we are also conditioned by our education system and society to take the safe path. We are trained to stay in the perimeters of the office, within the four walls of our cabins and be limited by the policies of the organizations we work for.

We are no different from these animals except for the fact that we are wiser than them. This means that while they cannot see the logic and evaluate the change around, we can. Look around you. Perhaps entrepreneurship was a big deal, perhaps impossible to pursue for many, but that was the truth during the industrial era. We are living in the digital age today. Things have changed. Conditions have changed. They are simplified. Starting a business is not an iron man's job any more. And yet, if we are still stuck in a job even when we want to do something of our own, the reason is only our own fear.

Are You Like the Tame Lion?

The lion was still all-powerful and fierce. If it wanted, it was not difficult for it to run away and yet it did not. It was trapped, not by the chains or whips of the ringmaster any more, but by its own desire to seek comfort in life. Its life was not easy even inside the circus as it was not free to run as it wanted and had to live in a cage that it hated. And yet, the pull of the easy food as a reward was so strong, that it would no longer chase a real deer. It lost its opportunity to craft its own future and settled for mediocre results that were way below its worth. In the process, it felt inadequate most times in life without knowing the reasons!

Something similar happens to you when you get too attached to your reward that comes to you in the form of a salary. You no longer want to chase the deer, i.e., the big opportunities out there that you are really worthy of, but only settle down to follow your bosses because they will give you a reward in exchange.

We are conditioned by the rewards, which is why we behave like trained lions. We are so well-trained in the corporate arena that even if we were asked to stay a little longer in the office and leave our families stranded, we would willingly follow the orders of our employers and keep working for the month-end reward. We keep saying that life has become boring, but we never quite realize that boredom is actually our choice. We chose to not play the exciting game of chasing the deer but opted to follow the command that came with a monthly reward.

So, where do we head from here? Stay tamed and keep giving lame excuses or take a bolder step to build our own empires? While you may have enough logical reasons to stay where you are, you also have enough emotional reasons to get out of the trap.

So, are you ready to take the plunge? I guess you are still having second thoughts. Never mind, it is normal, and I too had my share of dilemmas. You might already know by now that you are trapped, and if you have picked up this book, you must also have a desire to have your own start-up. And yet, if you are not already on the path, something is holding you back. But what is it? That's a big question that you might need to answer before you can take control of your life. So, flip the pages to the next section where you will discover not just what is holding you back, but also the ways you can break the trap to start living a great life.

But before you go ahead, answer these questions:

1. What are the opportunities/things you have lost or compromised for your job? What stopped you from living a great life so far? What came in your way?

   _____

   _____

   _____

2. What are the things you want to do in life but are unable to because of your job commitments?

   _____

   _____

   _____

3. If you were to start a new business tomorrow, what would that be about?

   _____

   _____

   _____

4. List the reasons why you should stay on in your current job.

_____

_____

_____

5. List the reasons why you should change your path.

_____

_____

_____

6. What are the two stressful thoughts that show up in your life, often? What is the source of such thoughts?

_____

_____

_____

Key Takeaways

- When a reward becomes a regular feature, you get so used to it that you would not pursue your dream just to ensure the reward keeps coming.
- Your life is governed by your choice. If you are stuck in a job that you do not enjoy, that is also your choice.
- What is holding you back from embarking on an entrepreneurial journey is not any circumstance or other people, but your own inner programming (often fear). You need to conquer that.
- A lion, an elephant, a baby or a grown-up man or woman like you, everyone is prone to falling for the small gains in life and creating beliefs that do not always hold true.

- Your reality of today may be different from that of yesterday. Only if you keep your eyes and ears open will you observe the changes.
- Your past is not equal to your future unless you decide to live there.
- If you do not work on consciously crafting a new future, you will end up living a mediocre default future.

Free Resources

https://app.startupsecrets.in/ch2

Part 2: Discovery

Time to See the Truth

Chapter 3

Three Truths That Tied You

Don't you want to be your own master? The king of the jungle? If your current life is not your dream life, you might keep contemplating what to do and true happiness will always remain at bay. Would you want to continue like that? Whether you want to grow or not would depend on what you see as your ideal or dream life that you wish to live one day. Do you see the cage around you? Would you want to get out of the cage? Would you want to be in a position to take decisions in your own life on your own terms? Is your current job so amazing that you are happy and feel like you are living your dream life? If yes, great! Keep up the good work. But if it's not, you perhaps want to do something bigger. Perhaps you want to enjoy the freedom to use your crazy ideas to create something new. Whatever you think is your dream, it is not far from you—but it looks so because you are holding yourself back. So, let us find out how close you are today to your dream life.

Definition

A Dream Life: a life of meaning, purpose, joy, happiness, love, passion, success and fulfilment where you are 'alive' not merely 'existing'.

Think about your dream life. What does it look like? For a few moments, close your eyes and take a deep breath. Imagine yourself a few years from now when you are living an ideal life in which you are happy, content and have everything you ever wanted.

Who are you? Where are you? What do you do? What do you enjoy? How do you spend a typical day? See yourself walking, talking and living a happy life in your mind's eye.

After you have done that, open your eyes and write down the experience you just visualized in your mind:

What does a great life at the next level mean to you? How does that make you feel?_____

_____

_____

_____

_____

_____

_____

_____

_____

_____

_____

_____

_____

Now, read what you have written and ask yourself—is this possible with your current job? If it is, then write how long it will take you to achieve what you wish to. Now, list all the sacrifices you will have to make to reach that level while staying on the current path.

Is it possible with your current job? Yes/No

By when will your dream be realized? _____

_____

What do you need to change now to make your life more aligned with a great life? What needs to move?

_____

_____

_____

_____

What are you willing to let go or sacrifice?

1. _____

2. _____

3. _____

4. _____

5. _____

6. _____

7. _____

(If you need more space, feel free to use extra sheets or simply fill in the online form at https://www.startupsecrets.in/chapter2)

Now think, if instead of continuing on the same path, you took the path of entrepreneurship, would you be able to live your dream? How long would it take you? What will you sacrifice for that?

Possible with your job? Yes/No

By when will you realize your dream? _____

_____

What are you willing to sacrifice?

1. Job
2. _____
3. _____
4. _____
5. _____

(I am sure you do not need more space!)

You may say, 'All that sounds good, motivating, and even inspiring but life is not so easy. I can't just leave my job, throw away all my privileges and take a big risk. What would happen to my family? What if I fail? What if I am not made for this? What if I fail and then when I try to get back, I don't get a job? What will my family think? How will I arrange for the money? What if I am unable to survive? I have so many debts; will I not drown in them if I leave the security of my job?'

Oh yes, I am familiar with all your apprehensions because I have been on the same road. And yes, it was not easy for me to decide. I have already shared my story with you. Remember how many pushes I needed before I could step ahead and say goodbye to the old life so I could say hello to my dreams? And that is exactly why I now want to assist you in making an informed decision.

Because I was naive, it took me a long time to launch my own enterprise. I could have taken that step earlier. I was going to succeed, and I have succeeded. If only I had taken this path earlier, I would have succeeded earlier. It was only because of my self-imposed limitations that I was living someone else's dream and not mine. People learn from their mistakes. I did, too, but wiser are those people who do not wait for their lives to teach them lessons the hard way, but are willing to learn from the mistakes of others.

'In life and in business, if you learn from your mistakes, you are "wise"; if not, you are "otherwise". It's only when you learn from others' mistakes and experiences, you are "intelligent" or "clever". Take your pick.'

—Neeraj Kapoor

If you wait for life to throw stones at you before you take the step forward, you would be committing the same mistake that I did. If you have come so far in this book, you realize that life is already throwing pebbles at you. It is just that you have chosen to ignore them because perhaps they are not big enough. I was blasted in life. The stones got bigger and bigger day by day, but I could see what was happening only when a huge andesite rock was thrown at me. I tried escaping the trap when I was about to get drowned, but you do not need to wait that long because you can do it now.

I was lucky to wake up in time. If I had not faced that dreadful meeting with my CEO, whose words hit me hard, I would have continued performing in the circus. I was lucky to have faced the bad news and that too, in the year that was supposed to be my best year in the corporate world. On one side, I was overwhelmed by my achievements and was so proud of my capabilities; on the other, I could see that despite my best effort, the company did not value me. It was time for me to value myself.

Let me ask you a question—if your company faced financial trouble and had to downsize the workforce, what are the chances that you will survive and not be thrown out?

You know the game, you know the catch, and you also know the risks. You know that the current path looks easier, but it is not. You also know that entrepreneurship looks difficult but there are many around you already walking the path who have succeeded, which means you can too. You also know that entrepreneurship is one path where you can rise beyond your imagination if you are truly dedicated. By now, you have already thought of your dream life and may have come up with an idea that you want to take forward and make a business of it. And yet, I have a feeling that you may still need a little nudge to walk that wonderful path.

So, what is stopping you?

If you knew three truths, then you would know why, despite the desire for change, you remain undecided. These three truths have the key to understanding what is stopping you:

1. A comfort zone is addictive
2. Your mind is playing a game
3. You fear the unknown

Comfort Zone

Have you ever been in a swimming pool? If you have ever learnt or tried learning to swim, you may remember the first time your coach told you to jump from a diving board. It was the same water in which you had been flapping around for days and you had been swimming already. Yet, when you stood on that board from where you had to take the jump, you were nearly frozen and unsure if you could make it.

You were scared, not because you did not know swimming but because you had never jumped from that height before. Before this moment, you had been walking down the stairs to enter the pool. Walking down was comfortable for you, but jumping from the diving board was out of your comfort zone. Now ask yourself—would you really become a better swimmer if you had not taken that plunge from the top when your coach pushed you?

No learning is received without getting out of your comfort zone. Even science has confirmed this. Research conducted by Yale University on productivity says that if you do not go out of your comfort zone, you do not learn because your stability can seize the learning centres of your brain. Auren Hoffman, a serial entrepreneur, says that if you want to keep learning and growing in life, you need to be doing new and difficult things 70 per cent of the time. Unless you have some stress about getting your reward, you would not learn and perform better.

In an experiment conducted at Yale, a few monkeys were trained by the scientists to hit certain targets, and in exchange, they would get juice to drink. 80 per cent of the time, they succeeded. Now the monkeys were able to predict when they were going to get the juice. The activity was not challenging any more as they were able to predict the frequency of the reward they would be given. At this point, their brain activity was measured, and the scientists discovered that soon after they developed this predictive capability, the learning centres inside their brains went off. They were in their comfort zone with the juice-grabbing game and did not need to learn any more strategies to be able to succeed. This is what happens to us when we settle ourselves in our comfort zones.

When you were a kid, you must have learnt how to do math, how to calculate the sum of numbers. As you kept practising, you became good enough. Then came the day when doing a sum was no big deal and you were so comfortable doing it that you would easily use the skill while making a purchase from the market. You would easily add the prices of a few items that you purchased and had no discomfort. So, there was nothing new that you were learning. But imagine if you went to a kirana shop to purchase around fifty items. Would you still be comfortable adding up those numbers? Probably not, if you were not a math wizard. What would you do then? Would you get out of your comfort zone and still try to add the numbers? Most probably not. Instead, you would let the shopkeeper do the calculation for you and tell you the final amount to pay. You would never try to get out of your comfort zone even to calculate the amount you are supposed to pay while shopping. Even before going to that shop, you would not make an attempt to remember the fifty items you have to buy but would simply make a list on a piece of paper or your phone that you could refer to while purchasing. You do this because it is easier and in your comfort zone.

What if you followed the other path? What if you tried remembering the list of items in your head? What if you learnt quick math and always calculated the total cost of items yourself? You could have become Shakuntala Devi, the Indian mathematician famously called the 'human computer', who was a master of numbers and even won against a supercomputer. Learning does not happen in the comfort zone but always outside of it.

How do we define the comfort zone? How do we know the limits we must cross if we want to learn? Why at all should we learn something new? Why should we try something new?

Why at all should we try to break out of our comfort zones if life is going smoothly?

You might have these questions on your mind today, and you might not feel like getting out of your comfort zone. But think of the time when you were younger. Some years back you were a kid who needed to compete with fellow students to get a placement. That is why you strived to learn more to be better. However, today you could be earning well in a job and have stability in life, so you would not feel you need to learn more.

If, today, I asked you to start a business, you might say that you cannot because you do not have enough resources, you do not have the knowledge, or you are too late to start. The truth is that you do not want to start because that will require you to get out of your comfort zone and you will have to learn new things and new ways. Well! That won't be easy.

The limiting beliefs are set in your head. So you do not try to get out of your comfort zone. To achieve anything which is out of your circle of comfort, you will have to break through those limits. Unless you do that, you will remain stuck in the cage and never get out.

But how do we break from these beliefs? That is a question we will explore later when we find out more about how these limiting factors work, how they stop you from growing and how that can be changed. Let us first understand how our mind works and what role it has to play in shaping our beliefs or putting the limits on our thoughts.

Games the Mind Plays

Do you control your mind?
Do you control your actions?
Or does your mind control you?

उद्धरेदात्मनात्मानं नात्मानमवसादयेत् ।
आत्मैव ह्यात्मनो बन्धुरात्मैव रिपुरात्मनः ॥

Elevate yourself through the power of your mind, and not degrade yourself, for the mind can be the friend and also the enemy of the self.

Lord Krishna says to his friend Arjuna, that the mind is your best friend as a servant but the worst enemy as a master (Shrimad Bhagvad Gita, The Song of God, chapter 6, verse 5).

American developmental biologist Dr Bruce Lipton states that when your mind is controlling you, you are running on autopilot mode. An average person runs on this autopilot mode, controlled by the mind, like a sophisticated robot, 95 per cent of the day. Alternatively put, you are a human only when you are in self-control; else you are a sophisticated programmed robot. When in autopilot mode, we put no or very little cognitive[1] load on the brain to think consciously to do things.

Let us see how. Read the statements given below and next to them put down the first thing that comes to your mind in the situation.

Once you're done, write down a number which is the percentage of thinking you need to do before you are acting in each situation. This will define the conscious effort that your brain would make.

---

[1] Definition of cognitive: 1: of, relating to, being, or involving conscious intellectual activity (such as thinking, reasoning, or remembering). 2: based on or capable of being reduced to empirical factual knowledge.

(Sample) You got delayed reaching the office due to traffic. Your colleague asks you why you are so late.

Your immediate response: blame it on traffic.

_____

_____

Tick the one that's most appropriate.
Your response is:

    a. Thought-through
    b. Almost automatic

1) Morning alarm rings
    Your normal response:

_____

_____

Tick the one that's your most likely response.

    a. Thought-through
    b. Almost automatic

Cognitive effort: _____ per cent

2) You got out of bed
    Your normal response:

_____

_____

Tick the one that's your most likely response.

    a. Thought-through
    b. Almost automatic

Cognitive effort: _____ per cent

3) You finished morning ablutions and got ready for
   the office
   Your normal response:

   _____

   _____

Tick the one that's your most likely response.

   a. Thought-through
   b. Almost automatic

Cognitive effort: _____ per cent

4) You approached the elevator and went inside
   Your normal response:

   _____

   _____

Tick the one that's your most likely response.

   a. Thought-through
   b. Almost automatic

Cognitive effort: _____ per cent

5) You reached your car that will take you to the office
   Your normal response:

   _____

   _____

Tick the one that's your most likely response.

   a. Thought-through
   b. Almost automatic

Cognitive effort: _____ per cent

6) You are standing before your office door that has a biometric that you need to tap to enter
Your normal response:

_____

_____

Tick the one that's your most likely response.

    a. Thought-through
    b. Almost automatic

Cognitive effort: _____ per cent

7) You saw an email that says that a report is needed in an hour
Your normal response:

_____

_____

Tick the one that's your most likely response.

    a. Thought-through
    b. Almost automatic

Cognitive effort: _____ per cent

8) You have to start your day and decide your plan of action
Your normal response:

_____

_____

Tick the one that's your most likely response.

    a. Thought-through
    b. Almost automatic

Cognitive effort: _____ per cent

9) 1.30 p.m.: It's lunchtime in the office
    Your normal response:

    _____

    _____

Tick the one that's your most likely response.

    a. Thought-through
    b. Almost automatic

Cognitive effort: _____ per cent

10) The first item in your to-do list is done
    Your normal response:

    _____

    _____

Tick the one that's your most likely response.

    a. Thought-through
    b. Almost automatic

Cognitive effort: _____ per cent

11) It's 6 p.m., the time when your day ends in the office
    Your normal response:

    _____

    _____

Tick the one that's your most likely response.

    a. Thought-through
    b. Almost automatic

Cognitive effort: _____ per cent

12) Your boss suddenly calls you inside and says that you have to attend an urgent hour-long meeting
Your normal response:

_____

_____

Tick the one that's your most likely response.

    a. Thought-through
    b. Almost automatic

Cognitive effort: _____ per cent

13) Your meeting is over
Your normal response:

_____

_____

Tick the one that's your most likely response.

    a. Thought-through
    b. Almost automatic

Cognitive effort: _____ per cent

14) You get a call from home that you must fetch something from the market before coming home
Your normal response:

_____

_____

Tick the one that's your most likely response.

    a. Thought-through
    b. Almost automatic

Cognitive effort: _____ per cent

15) Your purchase is done, and you need to go to your car
     Your normal response:

     _____

     _____

Tick the one that's your most likely response.

    a. Thought-through
    b. Almost automatic

Cognitive effort: _____ per cent

M (Your mind is controlling you) . . . Count all the 'Almost automatic' responses and write your total count here:

_____

Y (You are controlling your mind) . . . Count all the 'Thought-through' responses and write your count here:

_____

Now, to find out how long you have been running on autopilot on this typical day, use the formula below:

Autopilot = M/15 × 100 = _____ per cent

So, how long are you running on autopilot?

How does your life look inside the comfort zone?

Imagine you are a child, sitting in a classroom. Your teacher asks you to get up and start reading from your book. First, she instructs you to read, and then, looking at the others, she says, 'No one speaks. Everyone must maintain silence.' What will you do at this point? Will you ask her if you should also read in silence? Or will you go ahead, follow the exclusive instruction given to you earlier, and read even when your teacher has not explicitly mentioned that you should not be silent and that only you should read aloud? Why would you not get confused?

Because, despite the explicit instruction to everyone in your class, you knew that it did not apply to you because the teacher had asked everyone to keep quiet so that you could read peacefully and others could hear you. Quite simple and logical, no challenge whatsoever. And yet, when we graduate from our colleges, we stop behaving logically and surrender to programmes given to us. We don't think we need to think logically; our thinking has often been ruined by the monotony of our jobs.

While working in offices, I have often observed people playing below their true potential and finding excuses for not doing something just because that was not told to them explicitly. However, when the same people were younger, they did not need explicit instructions because they knew how to think.

When we were in college, we were learning and jumping out of our comfort zones almost every single day. But when we got into the corporate world, we stopped challenging ourselves. We stopped learning and became stagnant, which is why our mind sometimes shuts off and doesn't think beyond the given instructions.

The idea of a comfort zone in our heads plays a very significant role and keeps us in our cocoon always, so we never want to get out. We think that we are consciously working and working hard, but the reality is that once we know how to do something, we immediately go on autopilot, and without much thinking, continue doing it.

When we drive a car for the first time, we are putting conscious effort to learn, but after a month, we are on autopilot.

When we take up a new job, we learn how to do things every day but after a month, we have fixed schedules and to-do tasks for each day so we run on autopilot.

When we are attending a meeting for the first time, we try hard to understand what is being discussed and take notes, but after a few meetings, we know what would be discussed and can even predict the outcome. So, we do not take notes, nor listen to discussions but only wait for the last few minutes of the meeting when the host would summarize the points. You are on autopilot, perhaps fidgeting with your mobile or just sleeping with open eyes till the end of the meeting, and even if you are noting down the points from the slides, you are doing it without conscious thought. You are a human on autopilot who is acting like a monkey waiting for the juice, and your juice is the time when your meeting gets over and you can go home.

For you to run so long on autopilot, you need to have a program running in your mind. And it does. A well-instructed program runs in your subconscious mind. And this is not true just for functional jobs but even in the case of subjective actions and behaviour. When we are walking on the road, and all of a sudden we see a car heading towards us, the self-safety program would be triggered in our head, and within seconds, we would move away from the path of the car.

Just as your body retracts immediately upon seeing danger ahead when walking on a road, you act immediately in any situation of life based on what you are programmed to think. Your response would vary from person to person, situation to situation. For instance, if someone shouts at you at home, most probably, you will immediately get angry and shout back. However, if your boss shouts at you, you will perhaps keep your mouth shut and just keep waiting for him/her to finish, and then promise to take care of the issue that was discussed. The same angry response would be repeated each time you have a fight at home. The same response of silence would be repeated every time your boss gets angry. You need no conscious thinking to respond in these situations because your brain has already been programmed to guide you.

You are running on a program saved in your subconscious brain. You act like a robot who cannot change the instruction nor the resulting action. Try once to give a calm and well-behaved response to an upset family member whom you would shout at earlier. You will struggle to maintain your composure.

However, there is an amazing truth about programming in your brain. The variables are in your control if not the program. The subconscious program makes you work according to some set patterns all the time, but it is rolled out based on the values you assign to each attribute it considers when taking a decision to act. If we were all programmed like robots and we acted the same way in offices, following the same processes, why do some people make themselves heard while others stay in silent zones? The answer lies in a simple truth. They change the parameters used to take decisions.

Do you know how tea is made? Wherever you are in the world, you would use the same process to make the tea, but will the taste of tea always be the same? What makes the change in the output? Think of the ingredients that you use for making tea. Based on what type of tea leaves you use, the amount of water you put in, the milk you use, the sugar you add, and how much time you put the tea on simmer, the taste changes. Also, you would notice no two people can make the tea taste the same even with the same ingredients. So it is with life; no two people would infer, learn and take the same set of actions even with the same stimulus.

In the same way, even our mind's programming consists of some ingredients or, in programming terms, we can say attributes that we can assign different values to. Based on the values we assign, our output changes, performance changes, and consequently, our life changes.

Programming (Your Mind) for Success

There are four key attributes or variables that impact the way you view your world. It's your mind's programming that includes: your world view, mindset, goals and confidence.

World view: Everyone has a world view that gets programmed in their heads. The world view is the way you see the world. Do you have a positive world view or a negative one? Do you think that the world is stacked against you or are you a person who believes that everything happens for the good and always has high hopes?

The most common world views are optimistic, pessimistic and pragmatic. Optimistic people believe in the good side of everything, including their own capabilities. They take the path full of challenges. Pessimistic people always find obstacles that prevent the world from getting better. They prefer to stay on the path that is tried and tested. Pragmatic people are the ones who take sides based on logic or rational thought. They take the path of least resistance.

Mindset: How exactly do you see others, the environment, the world and things around you? Is a positive or negative world view ingrained in your mind? What are the assumptions, truths and values fixed in your mind? Do you think that fate is controlling you or you have complete control over your life? Do you think that your happiness is the responsibility of your family or is it yours? The beliefs that you hold on to help you understand the world in a unique way. The set of these beliefs is what creates a mindset. It affects the way you think. It affects how you feel in different situations. It also affects your responses to these situations. Your mindset is behind every action you take.

Goals: Are your goals your own creation or is someone else taking decisions for you? Goals drive your life, so if they are self-designed, you would know where you are going. But if they are not, who is going to decide where you go? And if you do not even have goals, you would not move. Just as we cannot use Google navigation without putting in a destination first, we cannot move in life without defining a goal for ourselves.

Confidence: How exactly do you see yourself? Do you believe in your own capabilities, or do you think that you are lacking in skills, resources or knowledge? How confident are you that you will be able to follow through the routine in your job? Perhaps very confident—but how confident are you that you will be able to sustain it if, all of a sudden, you lose your job one day? Perhaps not very. Can you just take an unpaid sabbatical for a year without struggling? How confident are you of that?

How the Subconscious Programs in Your Mind Appear

In computer programming, there is a concept called 'loop'. A loop is needed when you have to repeat an action again and again. And when these actions are based on certain conditions, we use something called an 'if-loop'. The word 'if' adds a condition to your program which means that you will keep repeating the action till the time the condition is satisfied.

Imagine your mind as a computer program that is using the four elements we listed as attributes. This is how it would look:

If (World view = negative; Mindset = the world is stacked against me; Goals = made by others)
　　{From lack of confidence = 0 to lack of confidence = infinite
　　{Thoughts > Expectations
　　If (Expectations = not met), Thought (I am a failure!)}}

In simple words, when you work, you have some expectations in terms of the result of your performance. When they are not met, you feel like a failure. And when this happens again and again, it undermines your confidence so that no matter what you do, you are going to be a failure. If you have a mindset that 'the world is stacked against me', the idea of failure gains strength. You may develop confidence but not in your capability. In fact, you become more confident in the silly belief that you cannot do it. And when this program dominates your headspace, you are promising yourself doom.

Now, let us see what a positive mindset program would look like:

If (World view = positive; Mindset = growth; Goals = self-made)
{From confidence = 0 to confidence = infinite
{Thoughts > Expectations
If (Expectations = not met), what did I miss? Learning > Transformation > Upgraded thought} }

The program says that as you keep thinking positive, you will keep expecting success, even if your expectations are not met. Your confidence would grow with time till you have made it. These loops go on and on; technically speaking, they become an endless 'for' loop which becomes a self-fulfilling prophecy for 98 per cent of humanity.

This program of positive mindset is different. It does not see failure to meet expectations as an actual failure, but as an opportunity to discover what you could have missed in your considerations. A positive mindset program would help you learn and upgrade your thoughts so you can actually bring a change in your life instead of just complaining about it. With practice, this would lead you to becoming a goal-striving, self-activated dynamo seeking progress and prosperity on a continuous basis.

Fear of the Unknown (FOTU)

One fear that rules all other fears in your life is the fear of the unknown. A lot of people are scared of ghosts because they do not know enough about them; they have never seen them. Imagine if ghosts were visible and travelled all over the world, even sitting with us in our cabins, talking to us about how they feel to be dead. Sounds funny, right, but not scary at all. You do not fear Patrick Swayze in the movie *Ghost*, or the ghosts in *Ghostbusters*. You fear ghosts for they are unknown to you. You do not even know if they exist around you.

Similarly, you may fear public speaking because you have never done it. You are not sure how you would be taken by the audience when you are speaking. You are not even sure if you would remember everything you wanted to say and not miss important points. You might not know what questions the audience would ask and if you would be able to answer them confidently. As a first-time public speaker, you are easily crippled by these fears.

But the good thing about this fear is that it has a short lifespan and it disappears after some time. The fear dissipates after much exposure. Will the fear of public speaking haunt you after you have spoken on the stage a hundred times? No, right?

You would only keep fearing till you did not understand the audience, but after a couple of attempts, you will get to see the pattern of questions, types of audience, and you can make a clever guess on what your audience would look like, what they would think, how they would behave, what questions they would ask. You are no longer fearful and you have gained confidence. You may have some nervousness before speaking but that would be more accurately described as performance pressure rather than fear of public speaking.

This fear of the unknown is the same fear that you could be experiencing a few seconds ago when you were wondering if you should opt for entrepreneurship because you do not know what lies ahead. You may have heard hundreds of motivational speeches. They tell you that you can do it, you must do it, and that you can change your life if you persist. But nobody tells you what lies on the other side. What challenges you would face and what actions you would have to take. Since you can't clearly see or even visualize what is on the other side for you, the outcome is still unknown and you fear the unknown.

This is why, despite the capacity that you may have and the dreams that excite you, you might be reluctant to get on the bandwagon of starting your own business.

Where Does the Fear Come from?

The fear did not exist when we were born. In fact, on the contrary, we were curious to learn about everything and did not fear anything until we experienced an injury, or someone stopped us from trying something new, warning us that we would get hurt. How did this fear form in our head?

Hans Eysenck, a popular neuropsychologist, says that fear is never innate but is learnt through exposure and observation. As the learnt information keeps accumulating in our head, it gets stronger every time we are exposed to a situation of fear and so, we get conditioned. Psychologists have observed that children do not have a fear of snakes till the age of six months, but when they see adults responding to snakes with fear, they learn to fear them too. The fear is acquired. And then it grows so big that instead of just fearing the fire or electricity, we end up fearing everything that is unknown to us. As teenagers, we never feared a new subject, a new sport, a new class, a new teacher or a new city that we might have moved to. But now, we fear a job interview, a new boss, a move to another company, and above all, taking control of our own lives. Most people choose to live in fear more than they live. Remember the famous dialogue, '*Jo dar gaya, samjho mar gaya*' (The one who lives in fear, consider him as good as dead) from the Bollywood film *Sholay*?

Everyone who breathes does not truly live, some merely exist. There is a difference between existing and living.

If we could understand this fundamental fact that the fear programmed in our heads is not natural but acquired, we would also know that fear is not always justified. The good news is that by reprogramming our mind, we can get rid of this fear that is holding us back from accomplishing great heights. How we can do that is going to be discussed later in this book when I give you specific tools to change your life.

But for now, remember the three points we discussed so far:

1. The comfort zone is addictive, and without getting out of it, we cannot learn and grow.
2. Your mind is playing a game keeping you on autopilot mode 95 per cent of the time. To break this loop, you need to 'transform' your mindset.
3. You fear the unknown, not because the unknown is scary but because you have been conditioned to believe so. By reprogramming your mind, you can eliminate your fear.

Now that you know what is holding you back, the next thing you would want to do is get out. If there are truths about things holding you back, there are also truths that can release you from this hold. That is something we are going to discuss in the next chapter.

Before we move on, do this exercise:

1. If you were a person who feared nothing, what are the things that you would do and are not doing currently because of fear?

   1) _____
   2) _____
   3) _____
   4) _____
   5) _____

2. Now, take a look at the list you just made and try to identify one fear for each of the above that is stopping you from doing those things in life.

   1) _____
   2) _____
   3) _____
   4) _____
   5) _____

Recognizing your fears is the first step towards eliminating them. The next step is discovering what is causing the fear and then finding a way to eliminate that.

Key Takeaways

1. Ask yourself if you are sacrificing more when you are at a job than you would as an entrepreneur. Making a list

    of sacrifices that you are making or would make in both cases would help you see the truth.

2. The comfort zone is addictive because in your mind it appears easier than stepping out of it to bring changes in life even if they are positive.

3. Your mind plays games by keeping you acting subconsciously. 95 per cent of the time you are operating on autopilot mode without much conscious thinking.

4. Your mind runs on a program that is shaped by your perspectives about the world, your goals, confidence and expectations.

5. A big thing that is holding you back is the fear of the unknown. You are unfamiliar with what entrepreneurship would bring in your life after you take the step.

6. Identify the fears that are holding you back from doing what you want to do in life, and then you will be able to see how they work and how they can be eliminated.

Free Resources

https://app.startupsecrets.in/ch3

Chapter 4

Five Truths to Release You

Truth is the pillar on which our life stands, and yet, most of the time, we want to live in an illusion and do not accept it. Instead, we keep living with our 'belief system' (B.S.). These are false assumptions or myths that are not true, but you live life as if they are 'the truth'. And when you are living with this B.S. and give it a strong hold in your mind, you fail to see the truth. When our B.S. is wrong, we eventually end up with the wrong conclusions. However, we do not know that they are wrong because what we see is only the conclusion and not what causes the conclusion.

This happens because the B.S. is sitting in our subconscious mind. It is never questioned and any attempt to reason it out often leads to confrontation and conflicts, and therefore, no agreement. It's like you are trying to install the latest version of the CorelDRAW software on a computer with the Windows 95 operating system. It will never work due to compatibility issues. Also consider trying to open an MS Word file in MS Excel. This will not work either; not because the file is wrong, but because you are using an inappropriate program to open the file. But you don't realize that; you simply conclude that the file is corrupted. You never question the software and the operating system.

That's why we come to conclusions but the reasons never surface. This is like having two parts to your mind—the conscious mind performing on the stage and the subconscious mind playing the tune from behind the stage. Although you cannot see the mind playing behind the curtain, you are still dancing to its rhythm. What are these assumptions that are sitting in our head and how are they shaping our lives?

Rewriting Your Destiny

Your belief system leads you to have a set of thoughts. These thoughts, when processed in the environment around you, give rise to feelings and become words, your words lead you to actions, your actions become your behaviour, your behaviour becomes your habit, and your habit eventually becomes your destiny. If you are not happy with the results you are getting, you have to reverse-engineer this equation.

Belief $\rightarrow$ Thought $\rightarrow$ Behaviour $\rightarrow$ Action $\rightarrow$ Result

The Myths (False Assumptions) and the Real Truth

The Myth: Business is only for the privileged few. I am going to fail if I start a business.

The Truth: You can be successful in building a business when you follow the process diligently with firm faith.

The Myth: You do not have enough resources to start a business.

The Truth: You have a business idea that takes no investment and can be started in an instant.

How do we identify which assumptions are wrong? Which are true? Which are due to fear and which are the result of plain wrong programming? These assumptions can be tricky if you do not know the way to uncover the myth and discover 'the truth', which is very different from 'your truth'. You need to dig deeper into yourself to make the discovery—a real awakening.

From my experience and the lessons I learnt from my coaches, I can give you five hard facts or truths that will question some of your crazy B.S. in different ways. If only you could get them corrected, you will be on your way to break the job trap and launch your start-up immediately.

A lot of professionals might believe that they will work hard till they are forty years old and then take early retirement to find peace. The reality is they don't know if they will be alive till then.

The Myth: Money is the root of all evil.

The Truth: Money is energy to help you accomplish your goals in life.

As you continue to break the myth and accept the truth, you will start to attract more and more money in your life.

We already discussed how the comfort zone is keeping you in your job. The B.S. is that the comfort zone is there and that it can be lived in forever.

The Myth: To get my business started and to make money requires too much hard work and a lot of struggle. It's a lot of responsibility.

The Truth: The comfort zone is an illusion. It is, in fact, a zone of vulnerability that stymies your growth.

The moment you are ready to let go of the comfort zone is the moment you are ready for corresponding growth.

The Myth: Starting a business won't leave me with time for anything else. It will make me super busy. Moreover, government laws won't allow me to enjoy my wealth.

The Truth: Starting a business can open up a new world of abundant time and money that was hidden from your view so far. Most tax laws globally are created to nurture businesses and help them grow.

Your business is your key to success as the effort you are making facilitates your business growth. You pay taxes on the net income, which means revenues minus all expenses that you may have incurred.

Unfortunately, these secrets are not openly known to a lot of people and their struggle never seems to leave them in peace. But why does this happen?

Regression to the Mean

Our life follows the rule of regression to the mean. When we are in a job where we are unable to save sufficiently, we feel unhappy and hope that if we work hard and get promoted, things would get better.

We may get a promotion, earn more and be happier for a while, but as we move ahead, our lifestyle tends to move towards luxury, and our expenses increase. We are back to the same situation we used to be in. Despite earning more, we still have the same struggle for survival as our expenses have gone up. We are almost never able to truly break out of the pattern and always stay close to the average feeling of discontent, which remains a constant.

If we have a typical pattern that we want to break out of, do we really do something about it? Mostly, we don't. Despite the churn burning our fat, we do not want to take any bold action. And when it aches, we blame our fate. We blame the world and fight with it, not realizing that the bigger fight is within us and with our own mind.

But why do we do that? We will deliberate on this in a little while, but for now, let's dispel a few myths and get the facts right before we get there.

The 'Someone is There' Syndrome

Since the time we were kids, we were used to having someone take care of us. And this had such a strong halo effect on us that despite becoming independent, we still think that someone else is responsible for our current condition.

If not a person, it's God. If not God, it's the force of the universe.

So, when things go really bad, we are looking for someone who would wave a wand like a fairy godmother and change our lives. In the Bollywood movie *Kal Ho Naa Ho*, there is a scene in which Naina, the protagonist, is sitting near the window with her mother and younger sister praying to God for a miracle, while on the other side of the street is Aman, the dying hero who stood as a hope for them and later acted like a godfather by resolving all the challenges before the family. He resolved their relationship issues, helped them increase their business and even brought love into Naina's life. What a touching story—as if he was living only to make this family happy, and once his work was done, he leaves the world. This was a story and not reality. In real life, you normally won't expect someone to come to you and enable you to resolve your issues.

Imagine you always had certain strengths and opportunities but, for some reason, those remained hidden from your view. Now, as you are reading this book, you are becoming aware of this new realization and waking up to the opportunities that lie before you. The thought clouds are getting diffused and your future is starting to become crystal clear in this moment. Still, you will have to take action on your own. Because there is no one on this earth but you alone who is responsible for your life.

The Myth: I will get whatever is in my destiny. So why do anything?

The Truth: We are 100 per cent responsible for the quality of our own lives and no one else is. You get not what's in your destiny but what you work to get.

So, if we do not take control of our lives, nothing will ever change. Your life is your responsibility—take it on and you will be the master of your own fate; leave it and others will control your destiny. Imagine you live on a piece of land that has treasures hidden in the ground. Now, these treasures are there for you, but you won't get any of them till you decide to dig deep. Therefore, you get what's in your destiny when you work towards getting it.

The Fifth Truth

We have discovered four truths about life that challenge your current B.S. A fifth truth that I am going to present actually holds the solution to all your problems, and mainly the problem of your indecision.

You may be living with a B.S. that you need money to achieve success in business but the truth is the contrary. It is not the money that brings success, but it is success that brings money. If you are successful in your actions, money will automatically follow. Sometimes, success may follow money, but money always follows success.

Let us dig into these truths a little deeper . . .

You Have Limited Time

Imagine you had a magic money app in which every night as the date changes, you would be credited Rs 86,400.

But this amount would be available to you only for twenty-four hours. At the stroke of the midnight hour, your account would be reset to zero and any balance would be cleaned out. At the same time, a fresh credit of Rs 86,400 would be placed in your account. Every day you can use this money to purchase anything you want. What would you do? Would you leave the money in your app or use it all? Would you spend it in buying some depreciating assets or would you invest in appreciating assets? Probably, you will utilize as much money as you can because it would not be there the next day if you leave it in the wallet, but those assets would remain with you and either depreciate or grow depending on what you chose to do with them.

Time works in similar ways as this magic app. On any day, we have 86,400 seconds given to us by our creator, the supreme power. The very next day, the seconds are gone only to be refilled with another set of 86,400 seconds. If you let any of these seconds go, they never come back. Imagine if you could earn one rupee for every second utilized, would you make use of every second or let it go just like that? If only you had control over how you used every second of your time, what would your income be at the end of the month?

However, this may not always be possible, for you do not really have all the time for yourself. A lot of your time goes into activities that are mandatory to live, such as ablutions, eating and sleeping. Some seconds belong to someone else, your employer for instance, and a major part of what is left goes to your family. If you record every minute of your day, you will find yourself spending a fair amount of your time every day on the job.

Think about this:

If you have dreams and personal ambitions that you want to achieve, how much time do you have to commit to them after you have given eight to nine hours to office work, one to two hours to your family, eight hours to sleeping, and two hours to snacking and ablutions? Three hours, and if out of these three hours, you spend an hour travelling and an hour entertaining yourself, then how much time would you be left with in your day for your dreams? Hardly any, and with this limited time, if you try to build your dream, how long do you think you are going to take to make it real? Perhaps forever!

Being a circus lion, you know how to survive, how to get your physiological needs fulfilled, but when it comes to fulfilling your dreams, even that one hour which you are left with is insufficient. Perhaps, in that one hour, you will only keep planning for months and then every small action would take more from you. You will move at a snail's pace, and when you reach your destination, if you reach it at all, it will remain like a blur for a long time.

Write it down: How long do you think it would take before you are able to fulfil all the dreams in your life by following the path that your employer has pinned for you?

_____

_____

_____

Consider, you are secure and living a comfortable life where you get your reward at the end of every month except on that one fateful day when the world shuts down due to another pandemic or war and your organization closes or suddenly decides to fire you for no fault of yours. Then, you search for another job. You would exhaust your savings while in transition and then, you will get a new job and the same comfort of the salary and the perks that come along with it.

You will keep living the same routine of 9 a.m. to 6 p.m. and spending the time from your daily time vault without anything left for yourself. And on days when your work demands more time, you will squeeze in more time from your life, mostly snatching it away from your kids and family. You will feel sorry for them, but then, will you have any other choice?

Now, ask yourself if you are liking this life where your time vault is with you, but its control is in someone else's hands. If you are happy, congratulations! It's time for you to celebrate.

You can keep living in the circus, but if you are not happy then it is time for you to think about other options.

I am not suggesting that you leave your job and run out of your savings in an attempt to chase your dreams. That would be really foolish. But what I want to invite you to think of are the possibilities, and then create a foolproof plan that assures you a safe and sure way out of the cage.

The Race is on …

Do you remember the days when you were studying in college? You had high hopes and big dreams. That is how we all start and then, some of us get trapped in jobs. Some struggle to even settle down. Only 5 per cent are in jobs they like and only 1 per cent are living the life they dreamt about.

If we see graduation as the starting line of the race for an independent life, we can say that we all started the race at the same time and continued running.

Most of us continued running on the path created by others but 1 per cent thought, 'Why should we take the path that everyone is following?' And with that thought, they rekindled their youthful fire and took a leap of faith to venture out on their own so that they could command their lives the way they wanted.

Now, you could be wondering if the 1 per cent were lucky enough to get the opportunities and the realization soon enough to get out, so they were never really trapped!

The truth is that even they were trapped once. No godmother or godfather magically appeared before them to pull them out with the swish of a wand. They decided to do it on their own. They were not lucky to not face any battles. In fact, they have fought harder battles than others and yet, with determination and a never-dying fire, they persevered and succeeded.

Success doesn't find you overnight or even in a few days. It may appear like a few days or months of work to you when you see success shining upon others. If you take a close look at their lives, the seeds of transformation were planted long back. But you heard about them when they were already on the pedestal.

Facebook was not an overnight success for Mark Zuckerberg, and Apple didn't just become the most valuable company in the world with a market capitalization of over 3 trillion dollars as many people might think. It was not just an idea that popped up in their minds and became a hit. There was a lot more to their stories. Some things were lost, lessons were learnt, patience was tested, beliefs were questioned, and then they emerged as leaders, giving the world two of the most influential, popular and cool organizations in the digital age.

If you are stuck in a job trap and want to get out today, this is the right time. You are luckier than the ones who worked before you because they have already paved the path and know the secrets to growth. You can simply learn from them and grow much faster than them. These lessons were not available to them. They had to discover the principles of business success themselves. This is exactly why we see companies like Uber,

Ola and Zomato rising high in just a few years while earlier companies took decades to grow big.

People have turned their lives around in a year, a few years or even taken decades. Now, you may wonder how long it would take you. It all depends on your level of determination, the speed of action, amount of knowledge and the degree of your openness to learning. There is nothing that is impossible for you as long as you believe in yourself and venture ahead with dedication in the right way.

As long as you have a solid plan and you are using every second of your life wisely, you are not very far from success.

The Comfort Zone: an Illusion That Kills Dreams

Do you believe that you are living in your comfort zone today or are likely to get there? While it may sound simple, it's not easy. Zoning out is difficult and would make your life harder. So, you do not want to do anything that pushes you. But what if I tell you that you are actually breaking out of your comfort zone every single day of your life? You are just unaware of how.

Think of these not-so-rare situations and feel how comfortable they are and if these require you to step out of your comfort zone:

You are crossing a busy road.

Your boss is screaming at you.

Your spouse complains that you are not giving enough time to the family.

You are sleepy, but you have a presentation to make for the meeting the next morning.

You are driving a car in bumper-to-bumper traffic.

On most of these occasions, you are not in your comfort zone but then you adjust by expanding it. After a few times, what feels like discomfort soon becomes comfortable. Crossing a busy road would be difficult for the first time, and even a few more times, but after that, you will know how to cross it safely and you will not feel so uncomfortable. You might not feel relaxed and there would be a little tension, but you are willing to put up with it without much ado.

In the same way, when you are driving on a busy street, you would feel uncomfortable for a few days. But then you will adjust and get used to it because you know that you have no other way out but to adjust. You would feel less discomfort when driving on the busy road.

The first harsh lecture from your boss is not in your comfort zone but by the tenth, you would have expanded your comfort zone and you would be okay listening to your boss's scolding.

We act out of our comfort zones every day, and very easily our mind adapts and increases its landscape. But we never expand it deliberately. We do not choose but we use this power within us only when we are forced by circumstances. However, this does not change the fact that we have an amazing capability to expand and adapt to anything.

The year 2020 saw a major crisis because of COVID-19 and everyone had to start adapting to digital platforms to stay connected. Before the pandemic, videoconferencing was used by only a limited number of people. But then everyone had to adapt. In the beginning, it was very uncomfortable, but today, we feel at home with the technology. Mobile payment apps like Paytm and Google Pay earlier struggled to increase penetration, but now even a vegetable vendor uses them. If you were not a tech-savvy person before 2020 and hated mobile apps and videoconferences, today, you know that you are not the same any more. If you are like most others, by now you would have learnt to use mobile apps for payments, videoconferencing for meetings, and online courses for learning.

As a human being, you have an amazing capacity to expand. All you have to do is use it wisely. Entrepreneurship could be out of your comfort zone today, but understand this—when you decide to take the plunge, you have the power to adapt and expand your comfort zone. And within a year, business will get inside your comfort zone.

Having said that, how could you really pull it off? How do you step out of your comfort zone and get the idea of business going? Perhaps you can learn a few lessons from the crisis of 2020. Remember how you adapted to webinars:

- First, you became comfortable with platforms like Zoom or Google Meet or MS Teams and learnt how to login, join and use.
- Then, you attended a few sessions and even conducted some for practice. Then you got the hang of it.
- A few things that you could not figure out on your own were taught to you by your colleagues, friends and family members. Perhaps they even gave some amazing tips on special features like blurring of the background, using remote control screen sharing, and adding subtitles.
- You experimented with its features every time you used your favourite tool, and at times, even tried some others.
- And then came a day when it did not matter which tool you used—Zoom, Meet or Teams—you could operate them all.

That is how you learn new skills. It goes with everything, be it a webinar or a business. So, even for becoming an entrepreneur, you will have to learn, practise, experiment, get tips, and keep applying what you have learnt till you get the hang of it.

When we were little kids, walking itself was a daunting step, and when it came to negotiating the staircase, we needed monitoring from a parent to keep us from falling. But within a few years, we had no trouble running even down the stairs. Studying thick books was overwhelming to us in college but we still managed and graduated. Cracking that first interview to get a job was out of our comfort zone but we learnt to beat the odds. Just like we learnt everything so well in life, we can also learn entrepreneurship as long as we have the willingness to do it.

Please remember one thing—nothing changes in your life while you are in your comfort zone because the real magic happens outside it. So, if you want to become an entrepreneur, you have to learn the activities and traits an entrepreneur requires, and bring them inside your comfort zone. Because if you do not, the illusion of comfort will kill all your dreams. It is your choice—you can stay in your comfort zone and let your dreams die or step out to expand your horizons and be ready to chase your dreams.

Regression to the Mean Is Another Barrier or the Key

In statistics, there is a concept called 'regression to the mean'. It means that no matter how high or low the value of a variable goes, it comes back to the mean always. Our life runs the same way. No matter which high or low turns we see in life, at the end, we stay afloat. But how does this relate to your work life or profession?

You think that the more you work, the more your monthly income increases. You will keep growing and be better off financially. You work more, you earn more and you save more. A simple formula, right? Wrong! Here is what really happens when you work hard to earn more every month.

At the start: You are earning X amount every month. You spend Y amount each month, leaving a saving of Z amount. Z is your average saving. Let us call it your 'mean'.

This month: You get a bonus because you performed well. Your salary is now X + A. You are happy and want to have a good time with your family, so you plan a holiday.

Next month: You earn the same amount that you were earning earlier. But because of the holiday that you paid for, your expenses increase to Z + B. Subtract this from the amount X and you are left with only a small amount of that extra A.

Emergency: A medical emergency at home or that insurance renewal that was due eats into your budget. Perhaps it is the instalment of the school fees just a week away. And that little amount that had remained also goes poof! Now, you are left with the same savings, Z.

Promotion: You are pretty good at work so you get a promotion after two years and your monthly salary shoots up. Now you are earning X + A every month. But because you got a promotion, you decided to upgrade your lifestyle. Perhaps you bought a car and that added to the monthly expenses, B.

Family: You upgraded yourself, so your family would also want to do the same. Perhaps your kid needs a new bike. Or it's time for him or her to go to college. Amount C gets added because of that. And when you remove this from X + A, you are able to save Z and only a little more. But this little increase in your savings is not really making you happy, as in these two years, inflation has been on the rise.

So, where are you now? Still struggling? Perhaps you were wise and invested in mutual funds or systematic investment plans (SIPs), but how far would you go with them and how long would it take before you had to crack the savings again to deal with your life emergencies?

Some people who were poor got a chance to change their lives by winning a lottery or prize money in a millionaire show. They lived wonderfully with the extra cash they got, but within a few years, they were pulled down again and were living with the same earlier struggles. Their fortune was gone. This has happened to many winners of the popular Indian reality show, *Kaun Banega Crorepati*. What went wrong? They were crippled by the rule of regression to the mean.

So, if you are thinking that you will keep working hard for a few years and after that, you will take early retirement, I am sorry to say but this might not happen. Because while you will keep earning more every year, you will also continue regressing to your average saving every time because of a number of factors like mismanagement, emergencies or inflation, and your expenses will only keep rising day by day, never really giving you the freedom to breathe.

But Why Do We Regress?

Do you know how a geyser works? It has a thermostat that controls the temperature of the water. The moment the water gets hot and reaches its set limit, the geyser switches off automatically. Something similar is happening with you in your life. Your money thermostat is set at Z amount of savings, so any time you exceed this limit, your expenses will also increase proportionately to create a balance so that your Z doesn't change.

If you have to change your earnings, then you will have set your wealth thermostat to a higher temperature. Set it to Z + A and only then can you ensure that your extra efforts do not go to waste. How do we do that? This is something we will cover in the later chapters when I will give you tools for your new journey.

Your Life Is Your Responsibility

Sounds boring and heavy, right? By now you must have already got charged up with a lot of things that you have learnt from this book. Are they all clear to you? Or are you a bit overwhelmed and cannot recall everything? Why don't we take a break, but let us not waste it. Instead, let us have some fun and learning together in this break before we move on to our next truth.

Let me tell you a story . . .

Once upon a time, there lived two brothers and two sisters. They had a father who was a great scientist who could solve the mysteries of the universe and was very well respected for that. The father was very curious about how the human mind worked, and despite all his efforts, he was still far away from uncovering the real secrets of the mind. His obsession with science was the reason he also made his children pursue science. Out of the two boys, Dilip was a data scientist, while Raj was a robotics engineer. The daughter Chetna was a psychiatrist, and her sister Barkha was a biotechnologist.

This is how a typical conversation at home went:

Dad, while sitting at the breakfast table, suddenly had a question for one of his sons, 'Raj, I know you have programmed a lot of robots, but have you ever wondered if instead of programming robots to think like humans, you did vice versa?'

Dilip, who was sitting near Dad, asked, 'Why would you want to do that, Dad? Aren't humans better than robots?'

Barkha, supporting her dad's idea, tried explaining, 'Oh! Dad only wants to consider the possibility of programming the human mind for good, right Dad?'

Dad agreed, 'Oh yes, for sure. Imagine if we could just remove all those negative emotions like anger, jealousy and irritation from the human mind, how wonderful our earth would be!'

Chetna was doubtful about the feasibility of the idea, 'Every emotion has some significance in life, Dad. We cannot just let go of them.'

Raj turned to her and said curiously, 'What harm would it do, Chetna, if we actually got rid of one negative emotion such as anger?'

Chetna was eager to explain, 'Anger is one of the basic human emotions that has not just a destructive but also a constructive role to play. It helps in building personality. It is required for your survival and gives you control, energy and motivation to deal with really threatening situations. It . . .'

Raj interrupted her, 'But if no one ever got angry, there won't ever be a need to play the survival game. So, if we find a way to chuck anger out of humans, we could all be at peace.'

Dad jumped in with a wide and happy smile on his face, 'You read my mind, Raj. I love the idea. Let us work together on a program that removes anger from the human mind.'

The discussion veered towards the possibility of an upcoming experiment, and Barkha was scared of what would happen next, 'And who will be the guinea pig this time? Consider me out!' She tried to get out of the experiment before she was roped in. The last experiment done on her was when her father tried to draw the data from her body to feed a robot. While the aim of the experiment was to make the robot her friend, it got so obsessed instead that it would follow her even to the washroom and to her dates. That was really irritating, and she did not want anything like that to happen to her again.

Dad assured her, 'Oh, don't worry, Barkha. We just need your expertise this time. How about Dilip?' Barkha sighed with relief. She looked at Dilip, who was frozen with half a morsel of breakfast coming out from his mouth. For a few seconds, he just stayed like that with only his eyes moving 180 degrees to see all the faces that were smiling because they were saved from becoming the guinea pig for Dad's crazy experiment.

In the next moment, Dilip quickly swallowed the remaining food and pleaded for mercy, 'Me, no, Dad, remember last time you did the melatonin experiment on me, I was unable to sleep for twelve days and then, I slept for twelve days. You stretched my bloody circadian cycle from twenty-four hours to twenty-four days.' Dilip should have spoken earlier. This was the penalty for not being an early mover in the crazy family discussion. In fact, he was a person who talked more with machines than with humans and was rather silent at most social gatherings. That was the reason he often became the scapegoat, unless he was required to be an active working partner in an experiment. Here again, he was caught and did not know what hell would break loose upon him with this new experiment.

Barkha commented, smiling at her brother, 'But did you not sleep well?'

They spent the next few days trying to eliminate the basic emotion of anger from Dilip's mind.

Barkha identified two compounds—$(HO)_2C_6H_3CH(OH)CH_2NHCH_3$ and $(HO)_2C_6H_3CH(OH)CH_2NH_2$—the chemical formulae for epinephrine and non-epinephrine. She extracted a reaction that could dilute these compounds to produce endorphins, the happy hormone, for which she needed to produce $C_{77}H_{120}N_{18}O_{26}S$.

Well, that wasn't easy and she needed help from her dad, who added the missing elements of carbon and sulphur in the right quantity to come up with a final reaction that would convert the emotion of anger into the emotion of happiness in Dilip's mind. Chetna was still of the opinion that this experiment needed to be tried from a psychiatric angle and a self-managed strategy should have been used. She was never in favour of playing with the chemicals in the mind. But who would listen to her?

Finally, Dilip was given the much-dreaded dose of a catalyst that acted as an agent to bring about this reaction, and within a few hours of the dosage, Dilip was found smiling at everything. Nothing seemed to disturb him from his peaceful state.

But the side effect of this peaceful mind was that he became insensitive to all bad behaviour and events. A horrible accident was shown on TV and Dilip's reaction was, 'Whatever happens, happens for the good.'

But that was not as irritating as his reaction when his boss told him, 'You are fired!' The boss was livid because Dilip was trying to convince an annoyed customer that his problem was not really big enough to get angry about. He said to his boss, 'You have fired ninety-nine employees in the last ten years and I make the hundredth. Isn't this amazing that you have reached a century in firing people?' The boss was really irritated by Dilip's reaction and insensitivity towards the job, and within a week, something similar happened at home as Dilip was able to annoy almost everyone in the family. Finally one day, Dad accepted that it was a wrong idea to kill a basic human emotion, and the family started to work on an antidote.

Why did I tell you this story? To remind you of the fact that everything you have inside you has a purpose, and in the same way, everything that is happening around you also has a purpose. You cannot just let go of the fear you have as it is needed sometimes. But not at all times. What you need is a balance. And to create this balance, you cannot use any shortcut. You cannot expect someone to come into your life and release your pain. You will have to do it yourself. Whether it is pain or pleasure, anger or peace, helplessness or resourcefulness—it is all inside you. If you want to create the right balance that leads you to success, you will have to take responsibility for it.

But, unfortunately, what many do is to shirk responsibility, and instead of accepting that we need to do something about the problem, we tend to hide things from our conscious mind.

Do you always mean it when you say that you are 'good' when you answer a routine greeting? Even if you are going through hell, you would not like to share the same with everyone. You may lie to others without inviting any repercussions, but if you are telling yourself that you are fine when you are not, then you would be doing an injustice to yourself as it was done to the character in the story I just shared earlier

Sometimes, you also know that everything not going hunky-dory in your life has something to do with your own mistakes. But if someone asked you why it happened, you would find conditions, the environment or someone else to blame. This will save you from embarrassment in front of others, but what about the injustice that you would be doing to yourself?

In psychology, this blame-shifting tendency is called deflection, which is both a clever and stupid technique to save one's face. Clever because by putting the blame on others, we are spared the beating, but stupid because by doing this, we would absolve ourselves from the responsibility and allow others to take charge of our lives.

Another major problem with blame-shifting is the adverse impact it has on the person who you are blaming. If the person is related to you, you would be weakening the bond, and if the person is unrelated, the trust would be gone. Next time, the person you blame would use the same tactic to put you in a trap whenever he or she gets an opportunity. Blaming creates enemies. It is not just the person you are blaming who would become your enemy, but you yourself would become your first enemy by letting your life be controlled by others.

Blaming is actually a natural coping mechanism used by people to deal with stress. A mistake makes you uncomfortable and puts stress on you which you try to push away by using a defence strategy. While this can save you from feeling anxiety for some time, it will not change your condition because you would be lying to yourself.

You may find it hard to accept your flaws because that puts guilt inside you, but in the process of saving yourself from guilt by blaming others, you will be putting yourself into a much greater danger by activating your tendency to self-destruct. You will destroy your relationships and your freedom.

Lying to the self is a much greater sin than lying to others. This is because that way you would be fooling the person who you should be most transparent with and give correct direction to.

But why do we do that? One reason is that we think that some person other than ourselves is responsible for our life and happiness. Since we were kids, our parents took care of all our needs and we were living in a cocoon where we were safe and never had to worry about anything. But as we grew up, things changed. If you have lived the life of a dependant for over eighteen or twenty years, how can you suddenly get out of the cocoon and start accepting your own responsibilities?

It is difficult, isn't it? But not impossible. In fact, you don't even have a choice because if you do not take responsibility for your own life, others will lead you and they may not necessarily ensure your happiness. So, the choice is not whether to take responsibility or not but whether you want to be happy or not. And who doesn't want happiness?

What Is Responsibility?

Responsibility is defined as response + ability; in other words, your ability to respond. Whatever life throws at you, you respond to it, and it is your chosen response that determines the quality of your life. But if you are not responding to situations but only waiting for others to take the lead, where do you think your life would go?

Let me share a simple formula for success with you:

Events (E) + Response (R) = Accomplishment (A)

In other words, you achieve an outcome only when you respond to an event. So, if you are choosing this response yourself, then the accomplishment would be in the direction you want. But if you don't, the accomplishment is not yours. Something will keep happening in your life, but it won't get you anywhere. The law of success is universal, and it doesn't change for anyone. There are no exceptions. This means that, in the presence of no response from your side, your life will be chaotic.

Imagine you are travelling in a car seated in the rear seat and coordinating with your subordinate over a mobile. The call keeps dropping and you try to reconnect every time it does.

You keep waiting for your subordinate to respond to this problem of frequent disconnection and he keeps waiting for you to do something about it. But no one does anything. What would happen? You will keep doing the stupid thing without any tangible result, and while you are still on the phone, you would get no tangible result from your conversation.

Now, think of this situation. Your call gets disconnected twice and you don't want it to happen a third time, so you tell your subordinate to wait for a while so you can try connecting with him through another mobile phone or an app that may connect. Will the problem be solved now? Will you be able to discuss what you wanted to? Will you be able to accomplish something?

As the boss of your subordinate, you might take the second route, but when it comes to taking the decisions of your life, you rarely take the lead. Instead, you look for someone to guide you even when they are not exactly the right people to advise you. And you do this because you do not want to take the responsibility for your own life.

Having said that, if you really want to take control of your life, all you need to do is—take 100 per cent responsibility. Not 50 per cent, not 90 per cent but 100 per cent. Take responsibility for what happens in your life, how you behave, how you think and even how you feel. You might say that it is easier said than done. How do I exactly do that?

The simplest way is to change your attitude. Right now, you want to play safe, but what if you were open to taking risks? You would not mind experimenting with life and would not be afraid to take the baton in your hand. And as you change your attitude, your altitude will also change because you will grow in maturity and capability to lead life your own way.

Remember, 'Your attitude will determine the altitude you will reach in life.'

Wealth Always Follows Success

Do you think that if you had a lot of money, all your problems will vanish? Most of us think that money can solve all problems and bring success in life. However, the truth is contrary. Success doesn't follow the money, but money follows success. This is why short-term gains like winning a lottery do not create wealth.

If you really want good money in your life, then you will have to set a foundation so strong that you succeed in life, and with this success, money shall flow into your life. Money is a form of energy that you get when you gain a skill that can make you succeed in your career or business. It remains with you forever, and as you keep using it, your wealth keeps growing every day. That is how we earn more money; not by using shortcuts. But what skill should you develop?

Skill can earn you a living, but it will get you wealth only when it is backed by a strong motivation that keeps you making creative use of your skills and overcoming any challenge that comes your way. But skill is a relative ability that allows you to do something effectively, which is why it does not stand on its own but is driven by an outcome that you wish to achieve by using your skill. This outcome is what keeps you motivated, not the skill. But what is this outcome? Many times, we think that the outcome we want is money, but money is only a by-product or a means to an end. The real end could be peace, comfort, fame, prosperity, authority or something else. Whatever is your end, it motivates you only for one reason—it gives you joy or happiness. So, in a real sense, your end point will always be your happiness. And what do you need to get this happiness?

- You need skill to achieve a goal that gives you happiness.
- The goal is what gives you happiness.
- To develop the skill, you need motivation.

Motivation, skills, goals—they all merge at one point, and that is your happiness. Then why beat around the bush? Why not grab happiness directly?

When you do something you love to do, it gives you happiness, and when this happiness overpowers the happiness you get from any other source, it is called passion. And when you earn from doing what you love to do, your passion turns into a profession, and with it comes the motivation without any effort. So, whatever skill you need, you will have enough motivation to learn, develop and use it to achieve success. While motivation can take many shapes and even money can be a motivator, it is only external and temporary. What comes from passion is internal motivation that never fades away. So, if you want to create success and generate great wealth, learn skills that are aligned with your passion. Follow your passion!

Don't Just Follow Your Passion. Have a Sense of Direction, As Well!

You must have heard this a thousand times. Everyone keeps saying it. But why? Because when you work on something with passion, success is about to happen because your level of dedication would be very high. You are not motivated by the external environment or actors but by yourself. If passion is what gets you happiness and most success, why do we run after money instead?

Since childhood, we are asked to study hard so we can get a good job and good money, and then we could settle down by becoming independent. Often, the most intelligent student in a college gets the highest salary in campus placements. That is how the bar is set. The money was the motivator and never the passion or skill.

Everything we do in life is to get good survival money. It is ingrained in our mind that money is the ultimate weapon that keeps you protected in life. Money is the need. Money is the goal. Money is life. With this programming sitting in our mind, how can we ever see anything else as more important than money?

Now think a little deeper. The most intelligent student of your class may not be getting the highest salary package or have become the richest in your batch. It's usually someone else. So, what carries more importance? Money or intelligence? Your company doesn't hire you on the basis of the amount of money you have put into your studies, but on the basis of how smartly you have answered questions in the interview. A poor but wise candidate will always be preferred at work, instead of a rich fool.

When you are taking up a job, you are not using money but your skills. The company in exchange gives you money. It is a trade between skills and money. That is the formula for wealth creation. If you have the right skill, you get the right money. Be better than others in your skill and you get more money. Get better at your skill over time and the company would reward you with a promotion.

However, a company is not there to just pay for your skills. They are there to create wealth for themselves and your skills are stepping stones for them to achieve their goals. So, they would not double your income for doubling your skill but would do a trade that is fairer for them so that they can earn more, spending less.

If we have to compare the employees who trade skills and employers who pay for skills, who would earn more? The answer is obvious and unanimously the same. Your company could be paying you X amount every month but the projects that the company will make you work on will get them 10X. If you are the best performer who gets them not 10X but 20X, then they will reward you by increasing your income from X to 1.2X. Get them 30X, and your salary will increase to 1.5X, give them 40X and you increase your income to 2X. Now, compare your success with their success. They achieved this huge success because of your efforts and perhaps the efforts of five more like you. All they needed to do was give you a small amount of their earning. You ended up giving them much more and yes, you were given only a small raise; I prefer to call that a few chocolate cookies.

You are earning a lot of money but not for yourself. You are working for your company and its owners. They are following their dreams, their passion and you are following them. They are creating wealth and you are creating sustenance. Does that ring a bell?

You are working hard to get them success and they are giving you money. So, while you are struggling to save money, they are getting money automatically as it is following their success.

Key Takeaways

- You have limited time in life. You cannot increase it but you can choose how to spend it. Do you want to use it to help other people reach their dreams, or do you want to use it to realize your own dream?

- You think that your job is keeping you in your comfort zone. But your boss can fire you any time. You would not always be granted leave when you want it. You will not always be able to take decisions yourself, and you may have to sometimes listen to some inappropriate conversations from your bosses just to keep your job. Are you really in the comfort zone?

- Human tendency is to follow a pattern that has ups and downs but your income always shows a standard mean. No matter how much more you earn in a particular month, the average would be maintained over the year.
- Your life is not shaped by any godfather or godmother or anyone who is supposed to be your provider. Your life is 100 per cent your responsibility, which includes your finances, your behaviour, your status and your reputation.
- It is not the silver spoon that you could be born with, but your attitude that determines your altitude in life.
- It is not success that follows money but money that follows success. This means you do not have to go after money but find success in your achievements.
- When you follow your passion, your mental battles are fewer and you can learn to win other battles in a logical way.

Free Resources

https://app.startupsecrets.in/ch4

Chapter 5

Five Keys to Unlock Your Hidden Treasures

In the last chapter, we touched upon the idea of happiness. In this chapter, I will take it forward because happiness is your ultimate goal in life. So, the first question that you must ask yourself when taking any decision for your life is, 'Am I happy?'

After you have put your hand on your heart, you will realize that your happiness is not just in your actions but also in your relationships. In a big way, your family is the reason for your happiness. Unfortunately, the same family that keeps you happy, safe and alive is the one that often, gets the least attention in the fight for power when you are working for others. So next, ask yourself, 'Does my family deserve my time?'

If you want to be happy and give time to your family, you will have to be free to control your life. But can you really do that while remaining a tame lion? Ask yourself—'Am I okay being tame?'

If your answer is no, it could be because you are not following your passion and your purpose in life. Without serving your true purpose, you can never be happy. But do you know what your purpose is? If not, ask yourself today—'What is my purpose?'

Lastly, when you know your purpose, your source of happiness and the key to giving the time your family deserves, you need to act and do the needful. And for that, you need not just aspire but also believe that you can do it. So, ask yourself this last but very important question—'Do I believe in myself?'

Happiness, family, freedom, purpose and belief—when you have them, you will have it all in life!

Are You Happy?

A simple question but the most difficult to answer. Just close your eyes and ask yourself—'Who do I need to BE to feel happy in this moment?' Answer this fundamental question and you will start to gain clarity about the actions you ought to take to be what you always want in life. Happiness is needed in life but is it also needed at work? Do you really need to feel happy in your profession? Time and again, studies have shown that a low level of happiness leads to a low level of productivity. There is a direct causal link between one's happiness and work performance because happiness is a powerful motivator.

But if you are still not sure why you need to be happy in your profession, here are a few reasons:

- It is not success in your career that makes you happy, but it is happiness that gets you success in your career.
- If you are not happy at work, what you get is not a promotion but weight gain, fatigue, headache and stress that leads to chronic diseases. It will give you a lifetime of pain.
- Unhappiness at work leads to work-life imbalance, which spoils your relationships and leaves you alone even in a crowd.

Researchers have proven that happiness-related constructs such as job satisfaction, safety and performance can impact not just your performance but also affect you deeply. While happiness keeps us motivated, the lack of it only drains us, making us suffer in every area of life and not just at work. When we are not happy, our work performance is poor. Our relationships are complicated. Our health deteriorates.

Now ask yourself—'Am I happy, in this moment?' If you are unsure of the answer, then there must be a gap in your life. This gap is the gap between 'where you want to be' and 'where you are'. If you feel that you are not fully happy, you might want to ask yourself, 'What will make me happy?'

Make a list of things that you must do to make yourself happy. Complete the sentences:

1. When I am at work, I feel happiest when I am …

   _____

   _____

2. When I am home, what makes me feel extremely happy is …

   _____

   _____

3. When I am out with my friends, the thing that makes me happiest is …

   _____

   _____

4. When I am out with strangers, what makes me most elated when I talk about myself is …

   _____

   _____

5. When I am alone, I am in seventh heaven when I am ...

_____

_____

When we talked about taking responsibility for your life, it included your happiness. So, instead of putting the responsibility on others to make you happy, take it on yourself. However, at this point, you could still hit a roadblock because, while you know the ways you can make yourself happy, inside your heart you may feel a resistance as you could be feeling that you do not deserve it.

Consciously you may say that you deserve happiness, but subconsciously there could be some guilt looming in your head for something you feel you have not done right. The guilt could also be due to your incapability to give enough time to your family. Entertaining yourself while your family is unable to can also create guilt.

There are many such small guilt trips that keep you away from your happiness. Some guilt could be big, such as for the times you were not there for your family or friend, or when you harmed someone for your benefit. For true happiness, you need to get rid of these guilty feelings. And to be able to do that, you must know them.

First, you made a list of things you must do to make you happy. Now make a list of things that make you feel guilty:

1. _____

2. _____

3. _____

4. _____

5. _____

6. _____

7. _____

8. _____

9. _____

10. _____

Having done that, take the next step and let go of the guilt. I am giving you a simple exercise that can help you get relief from big guilt trips. Do this, and you will feel relief in your heart:

Pause for a minute, pick up a notebook and write a letter to someone you have lost, someone you could not say many things to. You will say it now, through your letter.

This activity may even make you cry, and if it does, do cry. There is no weakness in crying. Crying is human. But it is important to do so because you need to have closure with people whom you have lost in your life. This can be your way of seeking forgiveness, or *prayaschit* (atonément), which is needed. Here is the format for your letter:

Dear _____,

I am sorry for _____

I forgive you for

_____

I ask for forgiveness for

_____

_____

I promise you that I will

_____

_____

_____

Does My Family Deserve My Time?

When I was employed in a job, I was preoccupied with the workload. Consequently, I could not reach my dad on time, but I was not going to repeat the same mistake again. After I started my own business, my schedule was in my control, and I could give enough time to my family as and when I wanted to. Yes, it takes hard work, too, and perhaps you have to work a bit harder than at a regular job. When you run your own venture, you are like a one-man army, but your life is in your control and so is your time.

After I started my business, I decided to spend more time with my family. I spent quite a lot of time with my mom as my business schedule was in my control. I could easily manage my meetings and engagements while also helping my mother at home.

Circa 2016. As days passed, my mom was getting weaker and more fragile. She became unwell and bedridden; she could only go from one room to the other in a wheelchair. Although she remained active with daily chores, her health was deteriorating. As an entrepreneur, now I had the privilege of managing my schedules, which I promptly did. My office was at Bandra Kurla Complex and commuting to the office daily was taking up two hours one way. With the traffic situation becoming complex, I decided to switch my entire business model to an online digital mode. The team initially had some reservations and hesitated but soon they were enrolled. Swiftly, we worked to ensure that every employee in the team was allocated a laptop and a data card, and in a matter of less than ninety days, we were managing business online on a real-time basis from the comfort of home. I was managing the business and giving time to my family at home, especially my mother. I remember, it was February 2017 and I was scheduled to participate in the International Yoga Festival on behalf of a client of mine (Govardhan Eco Village, the only UNWTO-awarded property in Asia). My mother displayed her desire to go to Rishikesh and I could fulfil her desire. Despite her frail physique, she was indomitable. She challenged me to go for the morning bath at the Ganga Ghat for seven days in a row.

A couple of months later, as we were having our dinner together, she said, 'You have done a lot for me, beta. I wish you to be my son again in the next life.'

I stopped munching, simply held her hand and replied, 'Thanks Ma, you are just a step away from moksha [liberation]. Why would you like to come back to this mortal world and get me back as your son? Wouldn't that be settling for less?'

It was an aha moment for her as she simply glanced at me with loving affection. That was the last evening I saw her alive. The next day, I served her breakfast and was planning to take her to the hospital as she looked weak. But she insisted that she take rest for a while. She loved spiritual music, so she asked me to play some. While I was adjusting the music player volume, she lay on the bed peacefully. Suddenly, I heard our domestic help calling for my attention. As I looked, I could see my mother lying still. In a few minutes, she took her last breath but with a smile on her face. She pointed at the lord while taking her last breath as if saying, 'It's time I meet Kanha.' She left me but she had no pain. Death is something that cannot be avoided. Everyone has to die one day, but I was lucky this time to have spent enough quality time with my mother and be with her till her last breath. I felt complete for I was able to make up for the mistake I had committed in Dad's case.

The excruciating pain that I had felt when I lost my dad was no longer troubling me as my mother had left peacefully.

I learnt my lesson the hard way, but you do not have to. Because you have a chance to learn from others. Lucky are those who can learn lessons from their lives but wise are those who learn from others. You do not have to go through the pain that I went through if you take control of your life.

If you are thinking that you cannot get out of your job cycle, you are living with a limiting B.S. because the truth is that it is not anyone outside but you who is trapping you. It is as if you have locked yourself in the bathroom from inside but are asking others to open the door for you.

No one is going to get you out when you have trapped yourself. No one can help you except yourself. So, if you think that one day a miracle will happen and get you out of your misery and help you cut loose, you are living in dreams that will never be fulfilled.

No one is going to be your godfather. You will have to help yourself and take a bold step to get out of the trap. But you can do this only if you realize that you are a trapped lion who wants to go on a wild hunt. But if you are happy being tame, then stay where you are—caged!

Am I Okay Being Tame?

Do you love your job? If you do, then you have every right to grow big by using your skills for your own business and creating wealth for yourself.

Are you tired or do you hate your job? If you do, then you have every reason to get out of the trap and start something you would love to do so you can create success and earn wealth with it.

If you are not even sure if you love or hate your job, consider that you are living with a fog in your head. And in the fog you can't see things clearly, not even where you are going.

Imagine you are driving a car in cold weather and there is fog all around. You have a friend sitting by your side who wants you to take him somewhere, but because of the weather, you are unable to help much. So, your friend suggests that you follow his instructions because he has a better sense of direction. You blindly follow his instinct, and wherever you end up, even if it is a ditch, it will not be your fault but your friend's, and the weather, right? When you are negotiating the job path, the job that you do not love, you are doing the same thing—driving on the instructions of your employer, except that your employer may not always be your friend. And if you end up in the wrong place, you would either blame your boss, the company or the work scenario.

But tell me frankly, despite the fact that there was fog, didn't you have the option of choosing your own direction? If your friend can show the confidence of knowing the way, if your employer can find a path for the company to go, why can't you?

You do not, not because there is no way out for you, but finding the way will take effort and perhaps make you a little stressed. It might be easy following the instructions of others while driving your life. But when you end up in the wrong place, you will realize that the comfort that you sought was for nothing, because the pain you would experience at the end would be far greater than the difficulty you could have faced while choosing your own path.

That's because by then, you would have given complete control to your employer. You will no longer be driving with instructions from the employer, but your employer would become the driver of your life. And that is when you are trapped like a tame lion who thinks that there is no way out.

As a tame lion, you will keep hopping between circuses, improving yourself every time to be a better follower of the circus master and putting up a better show. You will get more applause with every change of circus, but even after getting the largest crowds blowing you kisses, you are still that tame lion dancing to the rhythm of the ringmaster.

Can you stop this circus? Are you okay being the tame lion? Or do you want to get out? If you want to get out, the first thing you must do is find a reason to get out. Find your purpose!

What Is My Purpose?

'Would you tell me, please, which way I ought to go from here?' asked Alice.

'That depends a good deal on where you want to get to,' said the Cat.

'I don't much care where,' said Alice.

'Then it doesn't matter which way you go,' said the Cat.

This is a famous scene from *Alice in Wonderland*, written some two centuries ago by Lewis Carroll. It is relevant even today. If you do not know where you are heading with your job, you will not know where you will actually go. Your life will be full of surprises but not necessarily delightful ones.

So, ask yourself—'Do I know what my dream is? Am I sure that the work I am doing is going to take me towards my dream?'

If you are unable to answer these questions comfortably, you perhaps require a little nudge to get on the right track.

When you have to go to any new place and you use Google Maps on your mobile to set you on track, what question does the app ask you? It already knows where you are. But where you want to go, that is, your destination, is what it asks you to enter. It would not give you a path unless you enter your destination. Now, imagine you are walking the lanes scripted on the map but have no destination. What path will you take? Where will you reach?

You cannot start even a small journey to a shop without a destination in your mind. Then how are you living your life without any?

What if the reason you are trapped is exactly because you don't know where you want to go? When you do not know where to go, your employer is deciding the destination for you. So, you are walking the path, you are still using the map, but the map is not directed to your true destination but towards the destination chosen by your employer. Your employer is not doing you any favour by giving you a direction, but is only using you to head to the direction of his or her own goals.

So, by working for others, what you are doing is helping them reach their goals. There is nothing wrong with this, provided you also want to head in the same direction and it is not just the company that is utilizing your capabilities, but you are also using that as an opportunity to grow your capacities. But if the direction is not aligned with your purpose, you are doing an injustice to yourself.

What they are doing is just setting the destination, defining the path and then making you walk. You are walking, you are doing the hard work of hunting down the navigation path, but when you reach the destination, it is your employer who is actually reaching there. You are running like a ferocious lion, but your employer is benefiting from your contribution and you are a mere vehicle.

Then, when you reach the destination, the employer might choose you for some other role or simply bid you goodbye because your necessity might have ceased. This is the story of every other professional in the modern world. Sooner or later, they are left out and then they go on a hunt again—not for a deer but for another circus.

Everything that exists on this earth has a purpose to serve. In fact, every part of your body has a purpose. And if it doesn't, then over time, nature takes it away from you. Humans started with bigger, stronger bodies in size but when that was not needed, the size became smaller. If the necessity of something ceases, nature takes it away. And if the necessity of something increases, then the same nature adds to it.

We evolved due to these changes, by letting go of things we did not need and adding functions we needed so we could adapt to nature. If the law of nature itself says that everything has a certain purpose else it must not exist, how can humans be born without purpose?

But what is the purpose for which you are born? If you look at yourself individually, you may never be able to discover the truth. But if you see yourself as part of the big picture where your existence serves humanity and your contribution creates something that the world needs, you will soon realize that you have a purpose, and this purpose is much bigger than you ever thought.

You are not just a peg in a hole but you are the player of the board called life and your playground is this universe. You are born with a purpose, and this purpose is to create and contribute. But how do you contribute?

If you have to bring a big positive change in this world, if there was one way to make the lives of people easier or happier, what would you be doing?

Finding your purpose is not as easy as it sounds, and finding the path to achieve it is even more difficult because your purpose is connected with the universe, which is too vast. You have to look inside yourself, because inside is where the true connection between you and the universe exists. Begin with understanding yourself and then find your way towards your purpose.

Actually, a tricky question is, 'Who are you?' But do you have an answer? Who could be the person who knows more about you than yourself? And yet, why do you find it challenging to answer the very obvious question? In over thirty years of experience, I must have encountered this question so many times and I even asked thousands of people the very same question. Yet, every time, I sensed that people are often not clear about their true purpose or mistook it for playing small games. Almost every time, there was a struggle in answering it.

You can very comfortably talk about your company, your profile, your designation, your work, products and services, but when it comes to yourself, you fail miserably in answering.

You have a body, you have a car, a few possessions. This means that this body, your car and the possessions belong to you, but who are you, living in this body? Answer these questions honestly:

Who are you? How would you like to define yourself?

_____

_____

What do you stand for?

_____

_____

What are you best at?

_____

_____

What makes you different?

_____

_____

What keeps you going?

_____

_____

What drives you?

_____

_____

The answers to all these questions lie in answering one big question—what is your purpose of existence on this earth?

So, if you are struggling to answer the questions above, ask yourself:

- Are you here only because someone up there decided to make you or did he send you to earth with a purpose that only you can serve?
- Are you simply breathing and existing in your body or are you alive to make a difference in your life and the lives of others?
- Are you working only because you have to eat food to survive, which you cannot get without money, or are you working so that you can create a life of your choice?
- Are you striving hard because that is what you are supposed to do to be part of society, or because you are a dreamer who wants to achieve something big?

The mere existence of a human being without a purpose on earth is a cursed one. There is not a soul who is put on this earth without a purpose, and if you do not know what it is, how can you expect yourself to be happy? Do you really think that, without serving your true purpose, you would ever feel complete in your life?

An easy versus a purposeful life—this is the choice you are making today. The first option makes you a robot or a tame lion that runs on a program designed by others, and the second choice makes you a human who has the capacity to answer the simple but most important question: 'Who are you?'

Still struggling with the answer? Try another question: 'What are my dreams and desires?' If you are not sure of even this answer, let me help you by simplifying things.

Sit in a quiet place and answer the following questions:

- What do I want to accomplish in the next few years? What do I look forward to in the areas of health, business or personal life?

  _____

  _____

- If you were to contribute to the welfare or development of the world, how would you do it?

  _____

  _____

- What do I expect myself to be five years from now?

  _____

  _____

- If you have to be focused only on a few areas of business, where would you see yourself?

  _____

  _____

If you have tried answering all the questions and are unable to do justice to them, do not worry because the first step was to *start thinking* in that direction and you have done it. Congratulations!

Let us give it one more shot and this time, you will surely discover a few things about your purpose if you have not been able to till now. Make a list of twenty things you can be, do or have in life. Then add one more; make it twenty-one. You will begin to see that the initial ones were just superficial wants or desires. The real juice comes only towards the end. And after you have this list, think about what you are going to do about it. Make a list of actions that you will take to accomplish them. The first action that you would take towards what you desire to achieve should become your immediate goal. Now, subdivide the rest into mini action steps that you can take.

For example, if you wish to become a mountaineer, your immediate goal would be to get into shape. Subdividing this main action into mini steps, your plan would include:

- Join fitness courses
- Participate in marathons
- Do breathing exercises and meditation
- Educate yourself on fitness through reading

Write your list here:

1.	12.
2.	13.
3.	14.
4.	15.
5.	16.
6.	17.
7.	18.
8.	19.
9.	20.
10.	21.
11.	Selected:

The sequence is sometimes important but not always; just keep writing and at the end of it, read your list to see which one of the goals listed energizes you most. Don't think logically for this exercise; think emotionally—what would delight you most if you achieved it. Select that one, and then think of what could be the logical possible steps that would help you achieve it.

Sub-goals:

1.
2.
3.
4.
5.

Now, look at your plan—is it doable? Will you be able to achieve it? How much time would you take to reach your goals? Just like you create a to-do list daily in your office, you have just created a to-do list for your personal goals. But will they be achieved? From outside, on paper, it looks great, and you are sure that if you follow the action steps, you will be a super success in your goals. But how sure and confident are you that you will take the necessary steps and go ahead with your plan?

Let us assume that you are highly motivated and have a cool plan.

Spoiler alert! After a few days, you will see your list and you will feel like you are not going the way you expected or perhaps your plan sucks. And you will feel disappointed.

Why? Because you have missed something. And what is missing is coming from inside, not outside. While you did start with what you like, and you did create a logical list of things you should do, you missed three very important elements—belief, action and motivation (BAM!).

Belief that you can do it. Motivation towards a tangible result that you want to achieve, which is more than just having a liking for something. Action, the third and a key component, is what makes things possible.

When you cook a dish and find that it does not taste as good as you thought it would because it is mild, what do you do? Add a little salt, squeeze a bit of lime, and then it becomes perfect. You take some action to make things right. Till now, you have only listed your goals but haven't actually acted upon them.

Why have you not acted? Because action requires the right amount of motivation. To lose weight, you need an action, namely exercise. And to exercise, you must be motivated to do it; otherwise exercise would be very boring. Your motivation would not only be losing weight but the end result, which could be you getting a ticket to participate in a mega model contest.

Your to-do list only makes you feel the need to act, but it doesn't give you enough motivation to begin your journey or continue with it when you have to face challenges.

Now, think about your work life. Has it ever happened that you were working on a very difficult project and you thought you would not be able to complete it? Did you quit? You did not because your boss wanted you to finish the task by hook or by crook, and if you did not, either he would withhold your promotion, give you a bad review or worst of all, fire you.

This is like a sword hanging over your head that will fall on you the moment you say no to any task. If your organization gives you an unachievable goal, you will still work for it. Even if you do not know how to do it, you will learn and then work for it. If you encounter a difficult problem, you will find a solution for it and then work on it. You are willing to do anything that is required of you to achieve the target that your boss has set because there is a motivation—a negative motivation to not lose your job or position.

You are always serious about achieving your targets when working for your company, but when it comes to goals you have set for yourself, you largely falter and fail because you have no external fire to keep you on your toes. Motivation, whether positive or negative, works even if it doesn't make you happy. But a tricky thing with negative motivation is that it only makes you act and achieve the results asked for. It would not make you overachieve and go faster.

On the contrary, if the motivation is positive, you would not just perform at par but even go further. The negative motivation mostly comes from outside, but positive motivation is connected with the heart and it comes from inside. There could be an external agent motivating you, such as your guide, mentor or coach. But whoever the person is, the touch would be internal, and the words would be touching your heart. That is when you will be truly motivated from within.

Your dream is your biggest positive motivator because it makes you happiest if you achieve it. So, if you want real internal motivation, describe your dream in such depth that you can almost see and feel it in your mind.

Your dream would inspire you and make you forge ahead with motivation, and you will act. However, there is still something missing, the third element—belief. If you believe that you can do it, only then you can. If you believe that you cannot do it, then you cannot. It is as simple a law as that. At the start, when you are highly motivated, you will have a belief in yourself, but when things get tough, and they will—a little struggle will always be in your way—your belief will slowly start to fade. So, what should you do? Quit because there is a struggle? Or stay put because struggles are a part of life, and you can find a way to overcome them?

Struggles Are Opportunities in Reality

It is easier to remain stagnant than to grow towards achieving what you want because that path may bring on more struggles. But that would be only in the short run. In the long run, you will be much happier than you'd be if you had stayed on the easy-looking path you are on today. I can't put more stress on the importance of pursuing your dream but can surely say, 'You are happy when you are where you want to be, and you are not happy when you are not where you want to be.' Yes, you can't always be where you want to be, but there is a thin line between having a life of your choice with the struggles, and not having a life of your choice where there is no struggle.

Struggles are part of life, and they can't be avoided. But the fact is that most of us try to run away from these inevitable monsters, only to find ourselves in the middle of bigger struggles. A student avoiding the struggle of staying up late for studies can get into a situation where he or she gets bad scores; the bad scores would restrict him from trying for a job in a big company during campus placement. He would end up getting a mediocre job which he would not be happy with. The reason—avoiding short-term pain.

Your tendency to run away from struggles or difficulties is the most common reason why you do not achieve the things you want.

A young man who had recently joined an office was deployed to handle customer complaints and was given the task of rejecting or accepting them after review. His boss would not look at complaints too closely and would go ahead with whatever suggestion was given by the newbie because he was too busy to check. In the first month, the complaints received were standard ones and the fresher could take decisions easily. However, when things started to change in the company, more complex complaints were received. The boss had a good impression of the person who knew his work well, and the newcomer did not want to spoil his image, so despite facing the challenge of not understanding the complaints, he did not seek help.

He was too afraid to ask. This affected his performance, and soon came a case when he rejected a genuine complaint from a new client who was strategically important for the company. The client was very upset, and the account was lost. It was not just a loss for the company but also for the person who was responsible for the act. The newcomer was fired only a few months after he started. Had he been courageous enough to discuss issues with his boss, which he thought was difficult, he would not have had to face the bigger difficulty of losing his job. He was responsible for his own downfall. The reason was clearly his fear.

Struggles are only ways to test your strength, perseverance and your capacity to do something big. If success was easy and there was no struggle, everyone on earth would have been successful. There are names that inspire us; we love their courage, we appreciate their will, we discuss their stories, we become their fans, but we are afraid to take the steps that they had taken. We feel like this because we are afraid of difficulties. But can you say that in your life you have never faced difficulties?

Difficulties are a part of your life, and you cannot avoid them. You can do only two things—run away from them and put the responsibility of resolution on someone else or face them. In my view, there is one more choice even before you reach the stage of facing difficulties, and that is creating your own difficulties. If difficulties are unavoidable, then why not create them as per your choice? This may sound a little weird to you, so let me explain it with an example:

Nick Vujicic had difficulty in gaining acceptance from other students of his school when he was young, as he was one of the millions born without limbs. This was the difficulty presented to him by life. If you do not know who Nick is, you may find a lot of information about him on YouTube or in his book, *Life without Limits*. To be brief, Nick is a renowned motivational speaker, a person who was born without limbs and yet he could learn to swim and surf.

Nick set his own difficult tasks by wanting to swim, wanting to surf and live a normal life that a person with limbs would live. This looked impossible to others, and they thought he did not need to do this. But this was one difficulty he chose to create for himself which made him stronger than others could ever imagine. He learnt to swim and surf, astonishing the onlookers who would stand watching him with eyes widened at the mere sight of a person without limbs surfing like crazy.

Use your struggles, not as hurdles but as opportunities to grow, to be better, to be different and then they would not bother you but instead inspire you.

Do I Believe in Myself?

'*The secret of making dreams come true can be summarized in four C's. They are Curiosity, Confidence, Courage and Constancy; and the greatest of these is Confidence.*'

—Walt Disney

There are many books that will teach you to pursue your passion or transform your life in many ways. 'How to' guides are available for most of the professions as well as problems, but as you may already know, 'everyone is unique'. So, your problems or your dreams are also unique. The gaps you see in your life are also unique. For you, success may mean an entirely different thing from what others define as success. This is the reason most struggle to achieve things they want in life despite a large amount of information available to guide us.

The truth is that nobody can tell you what you should do unless you are clear about your own destination. They can tell you how to write, how to speak, how to use technology, but not how to live the life you want or what to do with your life. When you choose to have little clue of where you are going, you can easily say that your life is not supporting your dreams, or maybe someone in your life is not letting you live the life of your choice or even blame situations you find yourself in.

Whatever situation you are in, if you are always ready to label someone as guilty, without realizing that nobody has the power or duty to make you happy, change your life or help you reach your dreams, then you may end up choosing the easiest path. When things are not right, you may end up quitting or not doing anything about it. Get this: the journey to success is simple, though it's not an easy one.

One reason you could be choosing to remain where you are is that you feel the current life you are living is wonderful and comfortable, and what is outside is tough and scary. But do you really know what is outside of your comfort zone? Hard battles, yes, they are, but more than the external battles, you have to fight the inner battles that are harder. Your internal resistance supported by your friends and family is the biggest hurdle you have.

Whatever your reason, whatever your dream life, whatever your excuses, remember the old phrase: where there is a will, there is a way! Although a cliché, it has truth in it. It is only you who can build your willpower to accomplish anything, and I can show you ways to do that and the path you can take to reach the destination you choose.

Let me repeat one more time: the path is simple, not easy! When you are ready to take the path forward, go ahead and turn the pages to learn what exactly you would see on the other side!

When I Broke Free from the Cage!

I did not want to be a tame lion any more but a free one. So, after the discussion with my entrepreneur friend as mentioned in the first chapter, I found myself working on my start-up business plan and voila, many of my team members came offering to work for me for free till my company started making money. With tears in my eyes, I hugged each of them. We officially started a venture a few months later.

I was now an entrepreneur and I had my friends with me, the directors of a newly founded company. I was not alone. The universe was conspiring to make things happen for me just as it did for the little boy of *The Alchemist*, the popular novel by Paulo Coelho.

Whenever I look back at my life, I realize that 'failure' was one of the biggest stepping stones to my success and the reason for my transformation. While many of my other MBA comrades were still doing 'the right thing' by being in jobs, I was fortunate to discover my real purpose in life. If it was not for that one day when I got the deep realizations and clarity about my future path thanks to my boss, I would not be here. So, I would not call it a failure but the greatest gift. It is not wrong when they say that failure is a stepping stone to success because I have proof of that from my own life.

Today, I am living a successful life as an entrepreneur. I have crossed many significant milestones on the way and uncovered many secrets of success that I am sharing with you now.

From realizations to mind shifts, from planning to execution, and from no resources to accumulated wealth, I am there with you at every step. Just begin your journey and you will slowly begin to notice the transformation inside you. If you are in the rat race and want to get out of it, choose the less traversed path of entrepreneurship; become an entrepreneur. Do not think much and only surrender yourself to this book for a while and see how you emerge at the other end. I will be eagerly waiting to hear your stories of entrepreneurial success soon.

Key Takeaways

- You are born to live a happy life, and if you are not living it already, you are doing an injustice to yourself. If your job is the reason you are unhappy, it is time to find out.
- Your family needs your time more than you think, and if your job is keeping you away from them when they need you, it is time to think.
- You are a human, not an animal who should be tamed but you have decided to stay that way because most people go that way and are okay about being tamed. But are you too?
- Every human is born with a unique purpose on this earth, but only a few actually realize it. This is why they live a life without purpose and just keep going according to plans others create for them. Do you also want to stay a follower or do you want to find your true purpose?
- Struggles may bother you, but there is also a silver lining. Every struggle, if seen with a creative eye, can actually turn into a wonderful opportunity.
- Opportunities are struggles turned upside down by the indomitable will of the achievers.

If you do not believe in yourself, no one will. So, the first step to bringing a positive change in life is always to believe that you can do it and when you speak with a strong belief, others believe you too.

Free Resources

https://app.startupsecrets.in/ch5

Part 3: Action

Time to Take Control

Chapter 6

Why Start a Business?

Imagine you are sitting in your office cabin and you get a call from your mother who says that she needs you to come home. It's not a deathbed situation but one complicated enough for her to seek your assistance. You tell her that you will be there in some time as it's already evening, and you can leave the office.

After you disconnect the call, the screen flashes again. This time it's your boss's number. You know that your boss is going to ask you to do some urgent work which means you will not be able to get home fast enough to help your mother.

You have two options: 1. Dodge the call. 2. Pick up the call and tell your boss that no matter what, you are leaving for home.

Which Option Would You Choose?

Or did you just realize that you have neither of these options but only a third one—take the call and do what you are asked to do before you can leave. At the maximum, you will try to talk him out of it, but when your boss insists on urgency, you will do exactly what he asked you to do.

It has been long since you took a holiday so you decided to take a fifteen-day break. You booked a ticket to a hill station and flew there. On the third day of your holiday, your boss calls you and tells you that there is an emergency in the office and you are needed. If you do not come back urgently, it would mean a great loss for the company and you would be held responsible for it.

You have two options: 1. Politely reject his summons by reminding him that it has been a very long time since you took a holiday, and you deserve the break. 2. Tell your boss firmly that you cannot return and he should try to handle the situation on his own.

Which Option Would You Take?

Or perhaps, you realized that you have none of these options but a third one—to offer remote assistance to your boss, and if he does not agree, then cancel the remaining days of your holiday and book a flight back home.

You are at home, feeling really sleepy at night, not just because it's late but also because you have been working really hard for the past few weeks and have not rested enough. You want to sleep but you have a presentation to give to the client the next day and you have not yet finished preparing it because you need to add a few recently found details, which is taking time. You know you have to go to the office early because your meeting would begin first thing in the morning.

You have two options: 1. Tell your team that you will be a bit late the next morning and sleep. Wake up early and finish the presentation before leaving for the office. 2. Tell your client that you need to postpone the presentation by a day since you are still not ready with it.

What Would You Do?

Or did you just realize that you don't have the two options but a third one, which is stay awake to finish the presentation or wake up much earlier than usual to finish it in the morning before going so you can be at the meeting in time.

Have you now got the reason why you should start your own business? So that you can have several options—the option to live your life your own way, the option to make things work your way, the option to plan your life in a way that gives you time for yourself, the option to delegate some work so your business doesn't suffer, the option to take your own decisions.

Entrepreneurship may not be an easy way, but it is a freeway. It may increase your responsibilities, turning you into a one-man army but it will also give you complete control over your life.

But why do you need this control and freedom? We come back to the idea of happiness. Freedom gives you delight. Control makes you happy. And with freedom and control serving you, you can truly discover your real purpose, your 'why' behind starting a specific business. You already know why you should get into business. The next step is to discover 'why' you want to do a specific business.

What Could Be Your Big 'WHY'?

You could say that you have been at a job for years and you are sick of being trapped, which is why you should now have something of your own.

You could say that you are the master of your skills and have been very successful in your profession so you can start a business to make use of your skills for your own mission.

You could say that entrepreneurship is a golden egg and there are so many inspiring stories of people who could do it with fewer resources than you have, so you must start.

But these 'whys' will take you nowhere because they are thought from the logical angle, and despite some correctness in them, they do not have the positive motivational element that you need to thrive.

This 'why' is the most critical question for it gives us the goals, purpose, vision, policies and mission. An organization started with a powerful and clear 'why' sustains, but one without clarity often fails.

If it is clear that your 'why' is important, write your 'why'. Refer to the notes you made in Chapter 5 where we discovered what made you happy and what your purpose was. Your purpose is your 'why'. If you are still not sure of your 'why' statement, it could be because you have been trying to connect the dots with your conscious mind. But the reality is that your 'why' is not in your conscious mind but it is hidden inside your heart. So, connect with your heart and then you will make a real discovery.

Connecting with your heart would help you get a clear vision of what you want to do. And only when you have this clarity can you communicate your vision to others and pull in resources to start a business of your own.

Steve Jobs, the founder of one of the most successful organizations today, started his journey with a strong vision. The only reason his company became an immense success was that he knew how to make others see what he could visualize for the future. He could make others see the vision he had, and that was what made him such a powerful leader.

So, if you start off with a strong 'why', you will have the conviction with which you will speak, the confidence with which you will move forward, and the power which you will use to create systems and gather resources to give shape to your idea and shape to an organization that thrives.

You could get motivated by an inspiring speech or a moving life story and begin to question your choices. However, even when you have a desire to start a company and be the controller of your own destiny, you may still face the critical question of whether you should quit your job. You will have no clear answer unless you have your 'why' clear.

After discovering why, you will have to face the decision trap.

You could give yourself a push through motivational lectures and introspective moments. You would also have a wonderful and motivating self-talk like this: 'I am in this corporate role, I don't think this is the right thing for me, I want to do something on my own. I want to be my own boss. I am a free-spirited individual. I want to do something which fulfils my heart, and not just my company's goals.'

And still, you will remain in your thinking mode and will never take action. This is because you are unable to take that concrete decision and put your foot down to say, 'Come what may, I will start right away.'

While many reasons, justifications and empowering thoughts are staring at you, you are unable to take a step forward because you are trapped, not in the job this time, but you are trapped by your own mind that is failing to take a decision. You are in a decision trap.

On the one side there will be a nice 'why' statement that encourages you, and on the other side you will have arguments justifying why you should stay in the job. And when the two sides fight, the latter wins and you stay where you are. If you had to answer the question why you did not already start despite motivation, you will begin with a list of self-serving explanations.

Imagine you are locked in a room with four doors on each wall that you can use to go out, but all doors are shut by certain commands. These are self-serving explanations, frame blindness, short-sighted shortcuts and groupthink.

First Door: Self-Serving Explanations

The first command is that self-serving explanation that justifies your stay in the closed room. This is your 'why' again, but this 'why' is not for starting a business but for not starting the business and for remaining in the trap.

Second Door: Frame Blindness

Now imagine the same locked room; the first door is hopeless, and you try to take another exit. But even that door is locked, and the command is your mental framework that is still set on the job. Edward Russo, in his book *Decision Traps*, calls it 'frame blindness'. You are taking decisions based on a specific mental framework which serves specific problems that you want to solve.

If you are trying to solve your problem of money and you make it your 'why', you are creating a wrong frame and thus a wrong problem statement. That's because if money had to be the real reason why you want to start, you might take a few years to start because in business, you first need to invest before you see the harvest of money. You might see huge money but with time.

Your job is giving you instant gratification in terms of money, but business would not do so. If you create the wrong problem statement, you will be going nowhere and will remain undecided. Money is not your problem or solution to a problem. If you are unhappy with the money you have, this is only a symptom of a bigger problem which could be your inability to recognize your purpose in life or fulfil it. Your 'why' needs to be more than just a symptom.

Third Door: Short-Sighted Shortcuts

Now, let us get to the third door. You may have identified your key problem by drilling down your symptoms and then you will look for solutions to your problems. The first thing you would want at this point would be a fast way to reach your destination.

So, you will look for short-sighted shortcuts that can help you reach your destination superfast. Unfortunately, there are no shortcuts in life, and while you continue to look for one, you will find none and that will discourage you enough to stop every effort that you may be putting in to create the path to your dreams. The command to the third door is this short-sighted shortcut that is driving you.

Fourth Door: Groupthink

Now, turn to the last door and it is closed again with the command, 'groupthink'. This is the most dangerous one because it makes you rely on others to take your decisions. So, you speak to your family and friends to see if you should make such a bold move. What do you think they will tell you? They want you 'safe'. No one wants to get out of their comfort zone, and neither would they wish the same for you.

They are seeing you doing well enough, from their definition, and they would not want you to struggle. Also, remember the FOTU and the B.S. They have theirs too! Your family, too, feels the fear and is just as clueless as you are of the path. How can they guide you on whether you should start your own venture or not when they are themselves trapped and are not even fighting their inhibitions?

If you ask a person who is not an entrepreneur whether entrepreneurship is the right path to take, you will surely get a big no as the answer. If you truly want to know what entrepreneurship holds for you and if you are ready to start, look for advice from people who have done it themselves, those who are in business themselves. This is where a coach can play a brilliant role and help you see the possibilities. More than this, your coach can take you through an organized process of discovery of a real 'why', which will not be a mere motivational speech but a 'why' that will push you to get moving in the direction of your dreams, with consistency and momentum.

So, if you really want to take a decision, start with a stronger 'why' and flip the commands that are locking your way out so you can transcend the paradigms.

Flip Door One: A Specific Ask: Define specifically, what you want, why and by when you want it. You need to be resourceful to demonstrate that you'll be able to create it. Don't just want 'more money'. That's not good enough. Define specifically, how much, by when and for what.

Flip Door Two: Reach Out to an Expert: Who you listen to is who you will eventually become. Ask an expert who has been there, done that, who has the competency to help you, someone with the resources to help. Remember, whatever you want is already being provided by someone. Your smartness is in finding out those experts and figuring out how they can support you.

Flip Door Three: Add Massive Value: Now that you are learning from experts, model their behaviour. Do not be cheap on your journey to greatness. Do not take shortcuts. Simply model their business and you will start to see the results, and soon you will start to add massive value.

It is the combination of smart work and hard work that breeds success. Are you willing to put in effort and have long-term orientation and patience to wait for big results?

Flip Door Four: Assess, Evaluate, Course Correct: As you begin the journey, you are likely to go off on a tangent, hence it is most critical that from time to time, you assess your progress, evaluate it against the set objectives and keep correcting the course of action.

As you keep adding massive value, learning from the experts and modelling their business, you will start to generate happiness, bliss, better health, greater family relationships, and more wealth.

Key Takeaways

- First you make the choices and then your choices make your life. Every point in life presents you with an opportunity to take control if you make the right choice. Learn to make the right choices and your life will automatically start taking the shape you want.
- The first thing that you need to make clear in your head is your 'why'. Why would you want to leave your job? Why would you want to do something of your own?
- After you discover your 'why', you could still remain unmoved if you face a decision trap. The decision trap gives you more reasons to not do something than to do it. You could be using self-serving explanations,

short-sighted shortcuts, groupthink or simply suffering from frame blindness that keeps you from putting your foot down.

- If there is something blocking your way, make it go away by flipping your mental switch in the right direction.

Free Resources

https://app.startupsecrets.in/ch6

Chapter 7

How and When to Quit Your Job

Back in 2010, I had already served the industry for eighteen years and was earning a seven-figure income. When I decided to quit my job, I did not do groupthink with my friends or relatives, but I asked my friend who was an entrepreneur to guide me and then, as he gave me the answers to all the questions that were troubling me, I dived straight in.

The Initial Hiccups!

Diving in was exciting and adventurous but what happened after that was utterly confusing and crazy. While I did have friends to support me and resources to deploy, I had no concrete plan to venture ahead before I plunged in. I started learning and making plans after I had already quit my job. What was even more fascinating was the fact that I was trying my old job methods to get business, and they were simply not working. Yet I kept trying and trying with conviction.

I started from scratch and had to unlearn a lot of things that worked in my earlier jobs but would not work in business. I was going very slowly because most of the methods that I had learnt at my jobs made no sense in business. I had to learn a new way to give my dream a shape. And in the process, I struggled and made mistakes. For some time I felt like a failure until I found someone who was willing to guide me.

My coach opened my eyes to the blind spots that I was living with and shared with me that the reason I was failing was because I began my journey without the awareness of the laws and principles that worked in the business world. The way we succeed in a job was not going to help me succeed in business. We joined hands and he became my business coach. Now I was not alone and had someone holding my hand to help me learn to walk the entrepreneurship path. And with his step-by-step guidance, my business became profitable with higher revenues and better cash flows, and I began to see the light at the end of the tunnel. Actually, the tunnel transformed into a funnel!

My Discovery

As my business started to do well, the deep desire from within was not just to make it into another billion-dollar enterprise but also to enable other start-up entrepreneurs and aspiring ones to know the secrets and rapidly scale up theirs too!

After I had my share of growth, I looked around to realize that there were many like me, with immense potential who were still trapped in their jobs, and unable to take a leap of faith because they lacked guidance. My heart hurt to see that they were going to make the same mistakes that I had made earlier and would go through the same terrible circumstances. I wanted to do something about this and that's how Start-up Business Academy came into existence. That is how I became a business success coach. Prior to this, I was using logical reasons to stay put in my brand consulting business as a 'billion-dollar business catalyst' and then I found my purpose in life, which was to inspire professionals to manifest their dreams into reality by launching and rapidly scaling up their start-ups using the little-known secrets of billionaires.

So, if you are unable to discover your true purpose in life, don't worry. As long as you have discovered your 'why' for the business, you are good to dive in. After some time, you will get to know if your discovered 'why' is also your purpose on this planet or you have a bigger purpose.

Start with 'why' . . . go deep into it . . . discover your purpose.

And when your purpose is discovered, your 'why' rises to a whole new level from where no one can push you back. You will not need external pushes any more to move forward but would be truly inspired with your own mission in life.

As a 'billion-dollar business catalyst', I feel blessed to have enabled several brands on their journey from zero to over a billion dollars. It has been thrilling and fun. Now, I choose to wear another hat, that of 'start-up automation specialist' to empower committed professionals to unplug themselves from the matrix of corporate slavery by sharing with them the techniques to think not in self-serving, but purposeful ways. Consequently, this helps them to unlock their true potential and go on to build enormous wealth by using some of the billionaires' secrets that I have also learnt while working with four billionaire industrialist families of India on a one-on-one basis; namely, the Firodias, the Wadias, the Birlas and the Dhoots.

Without someone supporting and hand-holding you, it is not always wise to jump into business without any sensible plan to ensure your success. Because if you do that, there are chances of failing.

Your coach can pull you out of the deep end, what I call the death zone or the valley of despair. When you start your journey, you tend to make mistakes. But I guess you do not have to make all the mistakes if you are willing to learn from the mistakes of the people who walked the path before you. So, I would suggest you take a safer route where you create a solid plan and framework to take it ahead before jumping into the business arena. That way, you will have less risks and more chances of success.

Safe Way to Start

What I tell aspiring entrepreneurs is to not plunge into the business world without any backup because that could lead you to failure. You have a family to take care of, so you cannot be hasty about quitting without considering them. Instead of pushing you into the water, I would share with you a proven pathway to make a gradual and smooth transition from job to business. This includes step-by-step processes to make choices, gather resources, prepare for the journey, lay the groundwork, create concrete plans, quit the job and monetize one's passions. This book sets the basic structure for you to follow to build your dream company. Here are a few specific steps to simply get started with the next level of your journey:

Step One: Know What You Really Want

You can do this by asking yourself the right questions:

- What kind of lifestyle do you want?

  _____

  _____

- How many hours do you want to work?

  _____

  _____

- What kind of industry do you want to be in?

  _____

  _____

- How much money would you want to earn and by when?

  _____

  _____

- How would you use your money when you achieve your targets?

  _____

  _____

- What kind of a day would be your perfect day?

  _____

  _____

To describe your perfect day, you may write answers to the following questions:

- When would you wake up in the morning?
- What would you like to do the whole day?
- When would you work and for how long?
- How would you spend time with your family?

Describe your perfect day:

_____

_____

_____

_____

_____

_____

_____

_____

_____

The clearer you are in your head about what you want from life, the smarter would be your actual plan to achieve it. Your vision must be inspiring, achievable, believable and truly connected to your heart. By doing the exercise given above, you would have more clarity in the life you want to design for yourself.

Step Two: Find Your Ikigai . . .

Ikigai is a Japanese concept meaning your life purpose or your bliss. It is a sweet spot which can become your push button to start. It is formed with an alignment of four things: love, capability, need and ability to pay.

Love: It has to be something that you really love that comes from your heart, something you are also passionate about.

Capability: You could love music and dance, but are you extremely good at it and can you add value? You need to also have the capability to do well and provide a real contribution to the world in the field you love.

Need: It is not your need but the need of the world that matters, and if people have this desperate need which you can serve, you will soon be able to contribute. Discover how you can monetize your passion.

Ability to Pay: This is one of the most important elements that people miss out while working on the above three elements, and that is the world's ability and willingness to pay for your contribution. Now, you may call me an opportunist but let's get this straight. You want to create a monetizable opportunity that gives you a great life. Therefore, it's important that you choose a niche that pays really, really well. Or else you may get stuck doing a lot of hard work with insignificant results.

And when the four pillars are aligned, you find your ikigai moment!

My Ikigai Moment

Love: Helping people learn to launch their business and make enormous wealth.

Capability: I have had success stories with brands that made it to a billion dollars with ease and grace. I have had professionals who have been able to launch their new business within ninety days of my coaching without quitting their jobs.

Need: Professionals and aspiring entrepreneurs who want to get out of the job trap without having to fail or suffer and rapidly scale up their start-up businesses to a million dollars or more in two years or less.

Ability to Pay: As a 'billion-dollar business catalyst', I charge my corporate clients anywhere between Rs 10 lakh and Rs 12 lakh per day, but as a 'start-up automation specialist', it's less than that for a full year of hand-holding and enabling entrepreneurs to make a million dollars and more. It's like a sweet spot for my target audience.

Now, it's time to find your ikigai moment.

Love: _____

Capability:

_____

_____

_____

_____

Need:

_____

_____

_____

Ability to pay: _____

_____

Step Three: Build Your Business System

Your business model is the canvas that shows you how you are going to make money. Till now, you have been a part of the corporate world that had a way to make money, and that was through a simple exchange of skills against which you have been trading your time for money when you delivered on the milestones and followed the set of rules. However, how your employer really makes his money is never disclosed to you while you are at the job. If you are in a high position, you may have some clue as to how your company is making money. This can work in your favour, but if you are not in a decision-making position in your company right now, you will have a lot to learn.

However, despite your high position in the company, even if you know how the company is earning, you may still not know the complete picture of how the founders have made it possible. Running an already established business is what you have been watching at work, but starting a new one is a different ball game. From your founder, you would have heard only inspiring stories, but rarely would you know of their real struggles in making it to the top.

In a corporate job, everything is fixed as you have proper systems in place. Your salary is fixed, processes are fixed, key result areas (KRAs) are fixed and systems are fixed. But when you are becoming an entrepreneur, nothing is ready, nothing is perfect. Every day will be a lesson and you will have to keep trying different ways. If you keep the same mindset as you had at your job, you will fail. So, it is not just the technical parts that you have to learn but you also have to bend your mindset.

I remember years back when I bought my first car. Back then, I had not learnt to drive and here I was, becoming the owner of a car. Those were the times when there was a booking period for cars and one had to wait for months before getting delivery. I remember one evening I got a call from the dealer that my desired colour had arrived at the showroom and was ready for delivery. I did not know driving then, but my brother promised to teach me. So I learnt a few bits like starting the car, moving it forwards, and passed the driving test. I finally got my car and I was confident that it wouldn't take me long to adapt. The simple belief was that I had been a driver for long, although I was driving a two-wheeler and I understood road rules. But I soon learnt this is not enough!

On day one, my brother taught me how to change gears and then let me drive a little distance. I was elated and thought to myself that driving a car is cool. There was no need to balance it like a two-wheeler. One had to simply zip ahead when you wanted to. The night was a long one. I was impatiently waiting for the morning to get into my car and drive to the office.

Next morning, I got into the car. Put the keys in the ignition. My heart started to beat faster as I pressed the accelerator and put the car in first gear. The car moved forward, and I became consciously alive. Everything that day was so different. On my return home, it was like I was gliding through the traffic with butterflies in my stomach as I waded my way through. As I entered my building's gate, the feeling was no less than of a trophy waiting for me.

I invited my family to go to the temple nearby. It was a nice to and fro ride to the temple and back! 'I am a pro!' I thought to myself.

As we reached home, I asked the family members to proceed while I parked the car. Here was the catch, as parking required me to reverse the car into the stilt parking lot of the building and I had not been trained in reversing the car. I had watched people reversing the car and I thought I can do that too! I had no idea how to park a car because I was not trained to do that by my brother or anyone else. Pity that the two-wheeler riding experience didn't help. That was one 'big' mistake! Or an 'aha' moment. You decide!

To park a car is more technical than it sounds. You need to be aware of the front and back environment around your car, you need to know the operation of the reverse gear, and more importantly, the movement of the steering wheel and the handling of the accelerator and brakes. All this needs complete coordination.

I had simply no idea of all these complexities. I forgot to release the brake, put the car in reverse gear and pressed on the accelerator gently. The car did not move. So, instead of being gentle, I thought I should pump some power so it would move back. I did not realize that I had forgotten to pull the handbrake.

This time, the car moved, but instead of going back gently, it started swivelling around the axle and since I had pushed the accelerator hard, it turned so fast that it banged straight into the pillar of the building, crashing both the side door and the bonnet on one side. My car took a few turns smashing things, including my windshield that kind of cracked. I was screaming with horror not knowing what to do. At a little distance I saw someone running and shouting, 'Handbrake, handbrake.' I quickly pulled the lever and the car slowed down. I pushed the key and switched off the car, and after taking two to three big hiccups, my car stalled. I looked at my car. Just a few minutes back it was a wonderful shining beauty I was proud of, and now, it looked like a pile of junk metal in less than twenty-four hours of its arrival.

I learnt a big lesson from this incident. Never jump into anything without preparing yourself. And this is why I would never ask my mentees to push straight ahead but would help them chalk out a concrete, feasible and executable plan before they moved from their job role to an owner's role.

Plan for Your Big Shift

Before you start your business, you must be ready with your business model that you have thought through and is likely to succeed. Create a business model that has defined processes. Create your marketing strategy and find a way to reach out to a market that is hungry for what you have to offer. Let me give you a technique that you can use to create your plan for the big shift. I call it the FIBBGO Technique.

Find a hungry market
Build your business model
Build your marketing model
Go to market

Find a hungry market

If you have thought of a product or a service to start, think about the people who would be consumers. Will you have enough takers for it? Are they already consuming it in large amounts or are they on the lookout for it?

Build your business model

How would you earn money? Come up with a clear idea of how your processes will work, how your resources would be gathered and consumed, and how every activity will create value for your customer and a revenue stream for you.

Build your marketing model

Just having a product or service to sell is not enough. You also have to find a way to let your prospects know about it by putting it in the limelight. So, create an effective marketing plan to send out communication about your business to your takers in a persuasive way.

Go to market

Your business is ready, your marketing plan is ready, and you also know who your target market is. Now is the time you start executing your plans and take actual action by going to the market. Create not just a marketing strategy and business strategy, but an integrated strategy for the 'go-to-market' at this stage before you actually launch yourself into the market.

Quitting your job is never an easy decision. And it should not be a hasty one because, once you make that decision, your life will never be the same as before. You should go well-prepared. This transition of your professional life should not appear as though you are jumping from the frying pan into the fire! So, take the necessary first steps before you quit your job.

When to Quit Your Job

Now comes the big question: When should you call it quits from your job? The answer though is not standard and differs from person to person. However, there are certain broad patterns that you can consider to decide a timeline for yourself.

With the advent of technology as a big leverage, it's now possible to launch your start-up venture even without quitting your job. When you have ascertained your ikigai and have a proven model with an expert by your side, it's time for you to move forward and launch your start-up without quitting your job. It's not that you are not certain about it; it's just that you want to ensure that the money flow continues to grow in your bank as you push your dream forward into reality. The moment you start to see the revenue increases coming into your venture that are at your minimum sustenance levels, you are ready to plan your take-off from the current job. In the pages that follow, you are going to learn this in greater detail.

Key Takeaways

- Initial hiccups are common when starting anything. Even your job. Expect to face challenges when starting a business but remember that things will get easier with knowledge and experience.
- If you think that diving straight into a business is risky, yes, it is, unless you take a careful and safe path. Know what you really want, find your ikigai and visualize a business system.
- Use the FIBBGO technique to create a plan for your big shift to business. Identify a hungry market, build your business model and marketing model, and only then, have a go-to-market plan in place.
- Leaving your job is not going to be easy, and it should not be a hasty decision. First prepare yourself for the business and only when you are ready, launch yourself. But do not take too much time to make yourself ready and lose the opportunity to create a difference.

The best time to leave a job is not when you get your million-dollar idea but when your start-up starts to generate enough revenues that can sustain your minimum sustenance levels.

Free Resources

https://app.startupsecrets.in/ch7

Chapter 8

Take Your First Steps

Have you ever noticed that when you pinch one part of your body, your whole body twitches in a reaction? How does this happen? Our body is made of 70 trillion cells, and they are joined as a community to function as one. It is a brilliant system, but we never appreciate the fact that we are gifted with such a miracle!

We are like a mini universe in ourselves. There are so many things that are happening in our body every day that it is nearly impossible to even notice them.

In his book *Biology of Belief*, Dr Bruce Lipton, biologist and professor, says that the 'cell' as matter does not determine life but it is the consciousness within it which does. He once conducted an experiment and placed human cells in a Petri dish. He discovered something exciting.

The cells multiplied rapidly and soon reached the count of 30,000 cells, after which he divided them into three parts, in three different culture mediums. In one Petri dish, those cells became 'bone cells' and in another, they were converted into muscle cells. In the third one, they remained blood cells. While all cells were common, they changed shape because he changed the culture medium, or in other words, the environment.

This simply suggests that we have a tendency to become the product of our environment. Our bodies at cellular levels adapt to environmental changes. But how do they know when to change and how to change?

There are five sensory functions, namely, touch or the skin, taste or the tongue, vision or the eyes, hearing or the ears and smell or the nose. The sensory cells grab the information and push it further to receptor cells that take it to our brain which then interprets the signals, takes decisions and broadcasts the decisive message to the body. And this happens almost simultaneously, in fractions of a second with no conscious thinking involved. This is because it is all happening at the unconscious level. Though it's not legal in some parts of the world, we often find people talking on a mobile while driving without losing their focus on the road.

Our mind is not made for multitasking but when it does appear that we are multitasking, we are actually pulling together tasks that are using different parts of the brain. Often when we combine a cognitively demanding task with the process memory that is programmed into our subconscious, it becomes easy for us to take care of multiple tasks. Process memory is created by practice, such as learning to walk, talk and drive. Once we have a process memory created, it is never forgotten and is automated. Remember the part where I said that we act like robots? That is because of this automation of processes. Till the age of seven, we are mostly recording things to add to learning, and after that, we go on autopilot for most things we have learnt. In fact, we start absorbing the lessons from the environment even before we take our first breath in this world.

The story of Abhimanyu from the epic Mahabharata gives us an interesting insight into this. When the young Abhimanyu was in his mother's womb, he heard the story of the war zone maze

Chakravyuh from his father Arjun as he explained the strategies to cut through the maze to his wife Subhadra. But by the time Arjun reached the part of getting out of the maze, his wife fell asleep and he stopped halfway. Consequently, Abhimanyu, the little infant in the womb who was intently listening and learning the skills from his father, learnt only part of the process. After birth, as he grew up, this part of the education process remained incomplete for him for some unexplained reason. It is said that during the Mahabharata war, he got into the Chakravyuh with great aplomb but could not get out because of half-knowledge.

According to Sigmund Freud, our personalities are created in these early development years and never change thereafter. There is some truth in that, but contradicting it, many psychologists have spoken about the importance of the environment after childhood that also affects us and brings changes in our personalities, responses and thinking. As we keep growing, we keep changing and so do our ways of responding to the environment. But we cannot deny the fact that most of the programming in our mind is shaped by our experiences in our early years and these are determining most of our responses to stimuli from the environment. It is like the hard disk is carrying the previous impressions and the software programs of the past when we were kids and these are used to run the show later.

95 per cent of the time the programs running us are based on inputs we have received in the early years of our life.

While this fact makes our lives easy, it also makes it difficult because 70 per cent of those programs are disempowering and make you inflexible, or we can say, stuck.

When we have the environment pushing something on us, the reaction would be different for different persons depending on the programs stored in their subconscious. Since no two people are the same, their interpretations are different and so are their responses. But why am I telling you all this again? Just so you know that we are composed of programs formed by our experiences. But you also have the capacity to adapt and change them based on the changes in the environment.

If you are at a point where you do not think you can do it, it is not really you but the program in your head that could be doing the talking. Most of this programming is fed by common societal beliefs and your interactions with your parents. Now, you may say that your parents have given you this program so you can't help it. The good news is that you can always reprogram yourself.

So, your first step is to reprogram yourself. If your current programming is not working for you and not taking you towards your goal, it is time to upgrade your system. Your parents fed in the data decades back; don't you think that some of it would not be useful any more? If you were given a twenty-five-year-old laptop, would you be able to use it to do your current job? Or would you require some upgrades to it, maybe change parts or add memory? Or even change the laptop?

Well, you cannot change your physical body, but you can change yourself in many ways. And when I say change, I am not asking you to change your core but only your program that guides your responses. By changing your program, you will change your responses, and by the change of responses, you will change your destiny.

What Programs to Change

There are two kinds of people—those who see material wealth as happiness and others who see happiness as success. For the former, money is the most important thing in life, and for the latter, it is a by-product of what you do to gain happiness.

Which kind are you? What do you want from life? Money or happiness? What brings you happiness—health, relationship, intelligence or money?

There is nothing wrong in desiring money. Everyone wants it. Everyone needs it. But seeing money as a source of happiness will only get you away from happiness after you have toiled hard running after money and realized that it hasn't really got you anywhere near to happiness.

Seeing money as success and equating that with happiness is not uncommon because most people see it that way. This is because they are fed the same by their parents, friends, society and even co-workers. Whoever has money looks happy, and if you do not have it, you feel that once you get money, you will become happy too. But what if the reason behind their wealth was not exactly their desire for money but their desire for happiness, and as they became happy, they attracted more things such as money? What if this is true? If it is, you could be going on a completely wrong path.

The basic truth is that it is not the money that gives you happiness but the fame, name, friends and things you get from it. So, you are not truly running after money but after those things. But what if in your chase for money, you lose relationships, health and the motivation to keep going? Will you be able to enjoy that money?

So, if you are a person who really thinks that money is going to get you happiness, you need to change your mindset. Reprogram your mind.

In psychology, we have a concept called cognitive dissonance, which is a condition that occurs when our behaviour does not match our inner beliefs. The need for change is reflected by the feeling of unhappiness, but because of how we are programmed, we are almost never able to see this dissonance.

I once happened to see an English series, a twisted remake of the story of Jiminy Cricket from *Pinocchio* who was once a human child living with parents who were thieves. His parents wanted him to steal while people watched magic shows that the parents were putting up. Inside his heart, he was a pure soul, but he was programmed by his parents to be a thief. There was a clear mismatch between his thoughts and his actions, and this is what we call dissonance.

Once, his parents used him to kill a newly married couple. But after the deed he felt extreme guilt and experienced the highest level of dissonance which was killing him. At the time, he called for a fairy godmother who appeared before him with a wand. She asked him what he wanted, and he said that he wanted the dead couple to be brought back to life. She said that she could not play with the balance of nature, but she could help him change his life.

She asked him what he wanted to change. He said he wanted to change himself.

Then she asked, 'What do you want to become?' And he said, 'A cricket who never has to lie and is free to fly.' He was so fed up with the lies that he had to live with because of his parents that it looked much better to him to completely disown his human existence and become a cricket. And that was how he was converted into a cricket with a conscience.

Just like the boy in the story, we too feel those pinches in our hearts when we know that we are not acting according to our beliefs, when we are not following our true destiny. If we are programmed by the environment to behave in certain ways, we are also hardwired to sense the dissonance and know when we are not heading in the right direction. We always have the capacity to sense and change things, but we hardly ever use it.

We need to look back and ask ourselves what our definition of success in life is. Right now, you may have a myopic view of life because you are thinking within the boundaries of your programming, and not as a holistic person. If any one area of your life is not working, you may have a tendency to shift your focus to some other area and ignore the sticky feeling that you get because of your programming giving you pain. For example, if you are unhappy with a relationship, instead of looking at the programming that could be making you feel that way, you ignore the relationship and instead drown yourself in work or worse, alcohol abuse. This is how we react to a change in conditions when it is not favourable and requires us to change your programming. Changing it is a better but harder way, so we skip it.

Our common excuse is that we are doing it for our family, but are we really? Or are we doing it to avoid pain? With no realization or modification in your thinking, you will continue to live for twenty more years on the same program. Your focus will remain on the money that your company gives you, and you would keep working hard as you are doing now. You won't even bother to consider if you are truly getting what you deserve for the value you create for the world you serve.

You will keep earning some money, put it in a fixed deposit, perhaps invest some in mutual funds or SIPs and that is it. That is the maximum you can do with your current programming. But what if you change it, what more can you get? Not just more money but also more time and happiness. Would you like to change, then?

You need to change but what is the hurry? You may like that attitude, but the truth is that time is slipping by without you realizing it. Let me give you another story from a movie.

This is about a guy who chased money all his life and just wanted to become successful as fast as possible.

This man, who wanted to become an Ivy League professor, was pressured by his family to get married, for which he was not ready. He had a girlfriend whom he loved but did not want to marry because he wanted to focus on his career. One day while sleeping, he got to see God who offered him a chance to change his life by giving him control over time.

He could now fast-forward the unwanted parts of his life and jump straight to the happy moments. He was excited and used the power to skip ahead to the wedding. After the wedding, there was some bickering between him and his wife. He wanted to skip that, so he pushed time forward again and leaped to the day when they had kids.

Raising kids was difficult, so he skipped the initial years again and the kids became a bit older. But he was unhappy because the kids wouldn't stop disturbing him while he was trying to work, so he skipped time again. And then, it became a habit and he kept skipping years and years till he was on his deathbed. Then he realized that all those years that he had been chasing money and success, he had actually forgotten to live.

He did not remember the marriage of his daughter, had lost his wife to another man, and was now in bad shape and looked much older than he was.

The future is unknown, but you don't have to worry as it holds many surprises, which can be both horrifying and wonderful. But you cannot know what can unfold until you have lived it. So, for a moment, stop whatever you are doing in life. Think about what you want from life. What can you do to make your dreams possible? And what programming do you need to change to be able to develop the capacity to make your dreams possible?

As you are a unique person, different from any other person on this earth, I would not be able to tell you what programming you should change. But I can tell you that everything that is keeping you from chasing your dream needs to change. So, think now, and make a list of those bothersome thoughts, assumptions and programs that you need to modify in order to get to the next level and start your new journey.

1. _____
2. _____
3. _____
4. _____
5. _____
6. _____
7. _____
8. _____

Now, write down why you would change them. Or, in other words, write what possibilities will open up when you change the above patterns in your life.

1. _____
2. _____
3. _____
4. _____
5. _____
6. _____
7. _____
8. _____

When Are You Ready?

There is never a good or right time to start a new journey. But if you are drowning in work that you either hate or do not enjoy, it is time you stop doing that before it eats away at you. Instead of drowning yourself in 'learnt helplessness', you could proactively prepare yourself so you know for sure that you are ready before you take the plunge.

Learnt helplessness is experienced when you know that you do not have control over a situation that you want to change. For now, your current situation is that you may be in a job trap that you cannot escape because that will destroy your financial balance. The truth is that, despite your belief that you cannot change this situation any sooner, the reality is otherwise. The limitation is only in your head. And a way to get rid of this limitation is to replace the routine of the mundane job with the regime of Fo-So-Me-Co, which stands for:

Focused

Sorted

Meaningful relationships: building and managing, and being in the
Company of people who believe in you.

So, before you take a bold step, you have to focus on the outcome and action to get there. You are sorted about what you need to do to get there. You are building the right professional and personal relationships around you to keep you energized and moving towards your goal. And last but not least, stay in the company of those who truly believe in you.

You are the average of five people you spend most of your time with. This statement is a bare truth that can never be denied. The people we have close relationships with have great influence that can shape our thoughts about ourselves, about the world, about our job, our own strengths and limitations as well as about our goals. So, look around you and ask yourself if there is a goal that you are focused on. Do you have people close to you who would support you in achieving your goal or those who inspire you because they have achieved a similar goal themselves?

Make a list of the things you should focus on if you want to be ready to move to the path of entrepreneurship. Just as you pack your bags with all the essentials before you travel to a remote location, you must pack your head with essential thoughts, knowledge and skills. This would only be possible when you are focused on one big goal that you want to achieve. Then list all the actions you need to take in order to achieve your desired goal. Your list must be sorted on the basis of their level of importance determined by the extent to which they would help you reach your goal.

The One Big Business Goal that You Must Focus On

For example: Become a domain specialist—service provider or a manufacturer of the product that adds immense value. Now state your goal:

_____

_____

_____

Things you need to bring into your life to be able to achieve your goal:

Here are a few questions that you need to answer:

- What knowledge should you possess that can be useful for starting your business?
- What skills do you need to acquire before you start a venture of your own?
- What actions do you need to take to begin your journey?
- What resources do you need to keep the company of the right people who can assist you in your journey?
- What research is required to understand the stream of business you want to get into?
- Who are the people you would need to create a team that will help you execute your business plan?

Steps to Take

Imagine you have a great idea for a start-up. What would you do about it? Watch YouTube videos on how to do it? Perhaps find some motivation that could transform you into a person who is ready to walk the desired path? You may also take a few online recorded courses or perhaps attend some webinars. And when you have learnt from all this knowledge and heard or read motivational discourses, you would think you are ready to start implementing a few tricks and experiment with your idea. But, what is the chance that this will work?

About 90 per cent of start-ups that are formed fail, with less than 10 per cent making it to the fifth year. The reason is a lack of preparedness and understanding of how business works. Moreover, among those succeeding, very few are fast enough to capture the market when it is hot. Often the journey slows down for others while they are trying to figure out how business works.

If only they had the right guidance from someone who had already walked the same path, the journey would have been simplified and success assured.

Having said that, the first step that you should take is to learn about business. Try to get hold of a proven path with a mentor or a coach who is the right fit for your dream and is willing to hold your hand as you begin your journey, guiding you every moment.

If the value created by a typical start-up is plotted, it would pan out in the shape of a bell curve. It starts slow till the entrepreneur gets the hang of the business, it then spikes for a while and goes back down again. As the value suffers, so does the business and challenges kick in. The hand-holding by a coach could reduce the time you take to succeed.

Why having a coach works is because you get a model to follow the path already discovered by him or her. That is the easiest and fastest way to learn. When we are born, we know nothing about this world, and then we start mimicking our parents. That is a natural and biological way to learn, whether it is speaking or doing anything else. So, why not follow the path that works?

One of the gravest mistakes people make is that they spend so much time watching YouTube videos that just titillate their senses and make them feel they've already achieved something. The best you can do to serve yourself is to stop watching the videos and webinars that give you knowledge scattered so wide that it is almost impossible to put it into an understandable structure. Your coach could do that for you so you can take the appropriate action based on your 'why', your mission. Then you need to define the vision and the purpose, and contribute to the growth of the world through your business.

The first step is to get guidance and the next is to create a business model. Your coach can help you create one. But if you do not have a coach, you will have to do it yourself. What are the elements your business model should include?

Entry Strategy: How would you enter the market you want to cater to?

_____

_____

_____

_____

Plan or Lead Generation: How would you find prospects who have the capacity and willingness to pay for the products or services that you wish to offer?

_____

_____

_____

_____

Conversion strategy: What path and tactics should you use to convert your leads into a base of paying customers?

_____

_____

_____

_____

Delivery: How will you ensure that the delivery of your product or service is smooth for your customer?

_____

_____

_____

_____

Profits and Results: How will you ensure that between the expenses you have and the sales you make, you are able to create decent profits? And if any investment has been made, then do you have a plan for getting results and return on investment (ROI)?

_____

_____

_____

_____

Essentials to Complete Before You Fire Your Boss

As I said earlier, don't jump into the fire straight away, but be prepared. After you have answered the strategy questions given in the previous chapter, you will also have to think of practical aspects of creating business.

For a business, to begin with, you would need some finance; if not for starting, then for your survival till you start to make good money.

After you have the financing plan chalked out, you need to come up with a solid idea that would work for you considering your skills, capacities and market opportunities. Further, you also need to make sure that you have a plan for creating a team to help your business grow.

Financials

Job security is a great security, even though it is only temporary as you never know when things change at your workplace. In business, however, you sail through the hard times, and you find innovative ways to keep going till you are able to get your finances back on track. A job scenario is like riding a stream that ends in a waterfall, only you do not know when you will reach the falling end. Entrepreneurship, on the other hand, is like riding an unending sea that has storms but with a boat strong enough to ensure that you can keep sailing.

However, it is a long journey that needs you to pack supplies before you begin. The uncertainty can create anxiety in you and make you nervous. But if you have your finances planned well, half the battle would be won. Uncertainty will still scare you, but in a thrilling sort of way.

How Much Finance Do You Need?

You need only enough finance for you to keep living your life without losing your current lifestyle. The clothes you wear, the house you stay in, the time you give to your family—when you have enough to not compromise that, you have enough to begin your journey. Your business may or may not need your special financial support, but your life and your family do. Make no compromises there.

There is a certain fixed expense that you would need, to maintain your lifestyle. As long as you have budgeted for that, you would not have to take a hit on your self-esteem when you face initial hiccups.

Have some money parked to take care of the following expenses:

- A fixed budget to maintain your lifestyle.
- Add another 10 per cent to cater for inflation.
- Budget for school fees, holidays/travels, essentials, entertainment, subscription fees, mobile phone usage, etc.

Budget for a year, ensuring that the money you need to take care of expenses is with you in cash and not in blocked assets. Put it in a separate bank account and promise to not touch it unless it is required badly. You could have this money parked with your spouse, so even if you are tempted, you would have someone to keep you in check. The reason for not using it is to keep you motivated to generate enough from your business so you do not need emergency funds to sustain yourself and your family. But at the same time, having your money secured will give you a sense of security that even if you have to struggle in the beginning, you would not be compromising your lifestyle or the comforts of your family.

When you are secure, you are more motivated to take risks and more hopeful about things. After you have taken care of your personal and family expenses, then think about the capital that you might need for starting your business. In some businesses you may not need much and would be able to start with a small investment. But if you need more, then your next step is to ensure you gather that money in your account before you jump out of the old wagon.

Keep a budget to finance the requirements of your set-up like implementing a system, purchasing software, hiring team members and marketing.

Your Great Business Idea

Every business is created with not just passion but also with money in mind because business is about earning money. While you can choose the path that makes you happy, unless you have a plan that gets you a good income, it would not be a business that will thrive. A great business idea should also make great money because without it, you would not survive for long.

But What Is a Great Business Idea?

Your business is an extension of yourself, which is why to produce a great business idea that you can pursue and make it big, you need to start with yourself. Start with your purpose, mission, goals and objectives.

Purpose: Your purpose must always be bigger than you. Your purpose is something to do with the way you want to contribute to this world. Something that would keep guiding you in the long run even after you have achieved enough for yourself. Ask yourself what it is.

Write down your purpose here:

_____

_____

_____

Mission: Your mission is a way to reach your purpose, which would be in the form of a business. What do you want to achieve with your business?

Write down your mission here:

_____

_____

_____

Once your mission is defined, you could use it to generate ideas for a business. Your mission can be achieved in different ways. And each way can produce a different idea for your business. One way to draw out an idea is to go deep into your mission and chalk out what problems you are trying to solve for which you created this mission. Then, think about the assets you have, including financial, physical, social and intellectual ones. Consider them as your strength and the mission as your guidebook. Now come up with business ideas that would help you achieve your mission.

Once you have multiple ideas, evaluate them on the basis of your capabilities, interest, potential for contribution, sustainability, uniqueness, market potential, revenue potential, consumer benefits and feasibility so that you can filter out the one you really want to take forward. Select the ones that serve best in most areas.

Write your business idea by answering the questions below:

1. What is (are) the problem(s) your business idea would be solving?

   _____

   _____

   _____

2. Who is your target market and how would the consumers of your business output benefit?

   _____

   _____

   _____

3. How important and motivating is the business idea to you, considering your perseverance in case you face challenges?

   _____

   _____

   _____

4. Why is this business idea so important to you?

_____

_____

_____

5. How would the business idea get revenues and how much?

_____

_____

_____

6. Do you have enough resources or can you gather them if needed to set up or run the business?

_____

_____

_____

7. What will be the value proposition for your consumers or users?

To create a value proposition, you can use the following template:

I help_____

(target group of customers) solve _____

_____(mention the pain point) with my

_____

_____ (product/service/

solution) by_____(state the major benefits).

Once you are able to do that, you are ready to take the next step and define specific goals that you want to achieve by way of your business.

Goals: In the last section, you identified a mission and came up with a business idea. Now is the time to identify specific goals related to your business idea. While the mission is a pathway to the fulfilment of your purpose, it can only be achieved when you have clearly defined ways of achievement that you can call goals. So, using your mission as a direction, identify the goals you want to achieve by running your business. Your goals can be short term (a few months), medium term (one to two years) and long term (more than three years).

Start with long-term goals and ask yourself: What do I expect from myself in a year, two years or five years down the line?

_____

_____

_____

Where do I see myself five years from now?

_____

_____

_____

If the goals you just defined are achieved in five years, what will you achieve in the third year?

_____

_____

_____

If the goals you just defined are achieved in three years, what will you achieve in the second year?

_____

_____

_____

If the goals you just defined are achieved in two years, what will you achieve in a year?

_____

_____

_____

Now define your goals for the next three months.

_____

_____

_____

Objectives: Your goals can be short term, medium term or long term, but every goal would require you to do certain tasks and fulfil certain objectives, which when put together in sequence would result in the achievement of your goals. So, divide each goal you have identified into a few clear objectives.

Write your objectives here for the goals you created for the first three months:

_____

_____

_____

Now that your idea is in place, it's time to move ahead and think of the practical side of business. You need a team to work with.

Create Your Team

When you think of your team, do not just think of a team that would be working in your office. Also think of those people who would create your support system—your friends who will guide you, your family who will support you and a core group that will help you facilitate your business.

Get a buy-in from your family and relations first because they should not become your emotional roadblocks when you are trying hard to make ends meet.

You must appreciate the people you have in your life. They can become your support system if you have their buy-in. Even before you are starting a business, you are creating a foundation. It takes time and effort. Someone who has your interests at heart will be the person who will stand by you and cheer you as you make it.

The Virgin Way

Richard Branson talks about this in his book *The Virgin Way* amidst the stories of running the conglomerate and getting into multiple industries and businesses. In one of the corporate discussions, the participants were thinking of ways to eradicate HIV from the face of the earth. The question was: How do we control it?

Someone came up with the idea of getting into the condom business. The whole team was in consensus with that and started to work on it. Richard Branson discussed this new idea of selling condoms with his family over the dinner table.

The moment he mentioned it, his wife was stupefied and said, 'Ricky, I hope that was a bad joke. Can you imagine anybody buying a Virgin condom? It doesn't make any sense.'

According to her, the brand represented some values and should not be played with.

By that time, the Virgin Condom Team had gone through with the due diligence and was already invested in pre-launch activities. But Branson decided to cancel it, believing that it was not worthy enough. The brand would have got a very big beating in the market. That decision was the result of advice from his family. Imagine, if a person like Branson could benefit from his wife's opinion, wouldn't you too? It is important that you get a buy-in from your family on key strategic pointers. Their views can benefit your plans.

Once you have acceptance from those close to you, reach out to acquaintances who would matter in your business and who could support you, guide you, encourage you, facilitate you, refer you or pay you. These could be the people you know from the industry while you were working.

Make a list of them and think of them as stakeholders of the company you are planning to build. After you have done that, ask yourself if together they are enough to play the role of your support system. If not, who are you missing? There could be some more people who you need to be part of the team. Could adding a coach to your list help? Could an investor be of help? Could a technology partner be useful? Could a marketing partner make it easy for you to launch yourself? You might want to reach out to more people to broaden your list.

The list that you create would become your support system in the near future, but it would take long. To start immediately, you need a small core team that would include people who would be with you on the run when you are trying to build your business. Identify these core people who you can trust and who can be a great support. Share your business idea with them to get reviews and buy-in later.

They can also become a test market for your idea. Ask them if the idea that you are sharing would work. But make sure that this core team you are creating is not biased personally but is more of a professional team that has people experienced in similar businesses who have market knowledge that will be useful to you. Skipping this test can sometimes be a loss for you. It has been even for successful companies. You should be confident that if you go to the market directly and test the idea there, you could pull it off if it is accepted. But ignoring the brains that have more experience could mean you pay a price.

Test Your Idea in the Market

The opinions of your core group can save you from embarrassment, but even after that, you should first test your product in a small market before you launch it fully. When you do that, make sure you ask the right questions and are not carried away by your brilliant idea. Coca-Cola once made this mistake.

It once launched a new formulation of its beverage because in a blind test it was found to be the favourite of tasters. The survey result supported the idea. Finally, when it was launched in the market, the product bombed. The simple reason for this was that the survey questionnaire overlooked the defining question, 'If this new drink [formulation] were to be the only beverage offered by Coca-Cola in the market, would you go for it?' Instead of asking, 'If this drink were to be put alongside the original Coke drink, which would you prefer?' Due to this oversight, Coca-Cola took a beating and had to withdraw the drink soon after it was launched.

Prepare Your Mind for Your Business

You have come up with a beautiful idea and have defined specific goals and objectives you need to achieve in the coming months and years. But you would not be able to execute your plans unless you have the following:

Right mindset
Right toolset and
Right skill set

Your goals will give direction to your dreams but setting them too high could also be discouraging when you are unable to achieve them. So, be realistic when defining your goals. Also, goals set too high would not give you the confidence that you can achieve them. Your self-esteem would take a hit.

At the same time, you should not set your goals too low, thinking that you have limitations in terms of what you can achieve. The truth is that you possess limitless possibilities. Rules are set by society and systems for people and companies. Within the frame of these rules, there are specific guidelines and structures. But should they limit your ambitions?

Your capability could be higher than you think, but you will end up getting only that which you are asking for. So, instead of holding the limits created by others, be true to yourself when defining your dream about what you want to achieve. Anything is possible, only if you want it to happen.

We set our dreams, desires, goals and wishes in alignment with who we want to be. Competency, capability and skill set; everything can be developed in order to make that a reality. We believe that apart from the efforts and wants, there is an element of luck involved too. Having said that, even if luck is on your side, effort is still required on your part to make things happen. Actions need to be taken. And the action you need to take now is to start with your business.

However, your limiting beliefs could put you into a trap and you would keep having doubts. Your mind could play tricks and keep you thinking that you are still not ready, but the truth is that the next best time is now! Because the limits are only in your mind, which means if you think that you are not ready today, the answer will not change tomorrow. It won't change even after a year or after a few years. With doubts in your mind, you will keep thinking that you are unprepared until you take real action and get your plans churning.

No matter how great your business idea, how creative your goals and how feasible your plan, you would not get anywhere without action. And if you are thinking that you cannot do it because you have never done it before, remember this—experience is the best teacher.

Narayana Murthy founded a company called Softronics long before Infosys. Though Softronics was a short-lived company that lasted barely a year, it set a path of entrepreneurship for him to pursue.

But of course, you would not want to fail in your first venture. It can happen but not necessarily. You could reduce your chances of failure if you knew why and how companies fail.

How to Ensure That You Do Not Fail

Each year, thousands of ambitious entrepreneurs start new businesses. According to certain studies, these entrepreneurs are bright and full of passion but roughly by the end of the first year, more than 21 per cent of them fail. While another 30 per cent fail in the second year, less than 25 per cent reach the fourth year, and only 10 per cent of the remaining operate nearing the seventh year.

There are numerous reasons for such failures. These are the top ten:

- 42 per cent failed because the market didn't need the product at the time.
- 29 per cent ran out of cash.
- 23 per cent did not have the right team.
- 19 per cent were overshadowed by competition.
- 18 per cent faced problems with pricing or cost management.
- 17 per cent did not have a user-friendly product.
- 17 per cent started without a solid business model in place.
- 14 per cent were unable to market themselves well.

- 14 per cent ignored the needs, likes and preferences of customers.
- 13 per cent launched products at the wrong time.

Things happen when the time is right and when it's a best possible fit. Many times, it is not the idea that is flawed. It's the poor planning and execution that falls short! For you to be successful in your business, you need to have the right qualities of a leader and the right mindset of a creator. Here are a few qualities that you must possess:

- Be proactive with your actions.
- Always begin with the end in mind.
- Take small steps, achieve small targets and celebrate your small victories.
- Have a never-say-die attitude. Stay full of positive thoughts.
- Remember that you cannot work in isolation, so live with cooperation.
- Be open to feedback and open to unlearn and learn.

Free Resources

https://app.startupsecrets.in/ch8

Chapter 9

Create a Billionaire Mindset

Have you ever noticed the fine print written on the rear-view mirrors of cars? Vehicles coming from behind often look farther away than they are. That is why the fine print on the mirror states, 'Objects in the mirror are closer than they appear.' It's like a miniature representation of the reality, and hence it's important for us to know the right timing.

Something similar happens to you when you think of getting into entrepreneurship. It looks like a long journey before you can get the results you want. But the reality may not be the same. Your success may be much closer than you think, and if you want to be able to see how near is your destination, you need to first clear the fog in your head that is making it seem far.

But how do we know if the fog is even there?

- If you are unclear about where you are going, the fog is there.
- If you are not sure where you want to reach, the fog is there.
- If you do not know what you stand for today, the fog is there.

- If your current decisions are not making you happy, the fog is there.
- If you are unsure if the path you have taken is the right one, the fog is there.

How Can You Clear This Fog?

Remember the time when you first fell in love? You were absolutely conscious of dancing to the tunes of your beloved and doing everything to please them. You were alive and nothing else seemed to distract you. That is exactly what you need to do on your start-up business mission.

Fall in love with your mission and then you rise to chase it with the power of the universe which is ready for you to harness.

Universal Vibrations

Your world is shaped by your actions and your actions are triggered by your thoughts. But where do thoughts come from?

Thoughts come from a program inside your head that is created based on what you received from the environment. Since we began to learn in this world, everyone around us had an impact on us. With some we connected and we believed in them, their words and their beliefs. As a result, we absorbed their thoughts and created a space for them in our heads. We do not learn anything new, but we do add something new to existing information about something. That is what keeps adding vigour to our program and we keep changing our thoughts. As thoughts change, we keep changing our behaviour. It is like a chain that we are forming for every concept we have in our mind, while every link in the chain is inserted by a thought absorbed from a different person.

For example, our mother told us something about dogs—that they bark. Your sister who had an experience of a dog biting her added to it—they are dangerous animals. When you go outside, your friend pets a dog and says that not all dogs are dangerous; some are friendly. So, your concept of a dog is not just one thought, but a chain created not just by reading books or self-knowledge but by people around you. Your concept would now be—dogs bark and can be dangerous at times but some dogs are friendly. This formation of a chain of information is so automatic that we do not realize it but keep connecting the pieces to form mature thoughts and opinions. In psychology, this is called consolidation and is a proven fact.

This is a direct interaction in which we learn by the words of others and sometimes, we also absorb by observing them in experiences. But direct input is not the only way we make connections and interact with the world. There is another way that is more spiritual, more universal, more fundamental and more existential.

Did you ever have an experience of meeting a person for the first time and somehow feeling that this person could be trusted?

Did it ever happen that you wanted to meet a specific type of person and in the next few days you actually got to meet a stranger who was just the one you were looking for?

These are not rare but common experiences of many people that cannot be explained by sheer logic unless you believe that there is an invisible connection between you and other people of the world. Just like gravity holds us all together on this earth, perhaps the same gravity is also pulling us together following the rules of attraction. That is where the idea of the popular book *The Secret* by Rhonda Byrne came from—the idea of attraction.

But this is something you may have already heard about. Let us go a step further and understand how this law of attraction works on the ground.

Our body consists of cells and these cells vibrate at different frequencies based on the kind of thoughts and feelings they are associated with. Now, imagine that some cells in your body are vibrating at a certain frequency and there are ten more people in this world who have cells vibrating at the same frequency. What would happen? If you have studied science, you must have read about resonance.

The principle of resonance says that when two objects vibrate at the same frequency, their individual sounds appear to be merged and they both produce a unified sound. This means while individually they would make two different sounds, when put together they will make one unified sound. This is the principle on which orchestras work, for instance. Despite so many instruments played by different people in the same orchestra, you can enjoy the feeling of one melody. The music we hear in movie soundtracks is created using a number of instruments, but we hear one tune.

Something similar happens with our cells. When they vibrate in unison, they all get unified or connected, and that is how we are able to attract like-minded people in our lives even when we are living thousands of miles apart.

These universal vibrations can give us power to be more and achieve more in life. So, if you have a goal in life and need the right people who could help you achieve your goals, use this power of universal vibrations and attract them into your life. For instance, if you want to get a prospective client before you finally quit your job, start thinking about the client with a strong belief in your heart and soon you will find a likelihood taking shape. Without you even realizing it, the person you need will make an entry into your life, give you the opportunity to start a new business, and soon you will be in a position to bid goodbye to your job and start a new journey.

Your cells act like batteries that have both positive and negative charge. Based on what charge you use, you will attract things and people in your life. For example, if you think that you are stuck and will never be able to start something of your own, you will attract situations that will keep you from taking a leap. On the contrary, if you start thinking that you are actually free to leave your job and all you need is one client that you are going to get soon, you will attract a potential client who you will soon onboard and thereby start a new journey of entrepreneurship.

You can also compare this with a radio channel that broadcasts a message at a certain frequency. Every radio that is tuned on the same frequency plays the same message or song. Create the right frequencies in your head, and your head will start broadcasting it to the world like a radio. The right person and situation will then grab this signal you are beeping and will start vibrating with you.

Whether you imagine cells vibrating and connecting or radio channels creating signals for connection, the fundamentals remain the same—we can connect with the right people even when they are not already before us or in our lives.

While this is more of a universal knowledge, let us add some biology to it. When you start vibrating at a certain frequency, electromagnetic energy is created by your brain, and your protein structures begin to modify to build a creative consciousness that enables your ideas to reach out to the people you are attracting. It even tells you what you need to do.

The vibrations are so powerful that they do not just attract people but also create a navigational path in your head so you know where you will find the person you attracted. The same thing happens with the person you are attracting, who also gets a navigational cue, and the intention to meet is generated. That is how a connecting path is created, and you end up meeting. This works not just with people but also with situations and things.

It all began with a positive thought that has manifested into a desired outcome with the power of universal vibrations.

How Can You Use the Universal Energy to Create a Difference in Your Life?

For you to be what you want to be, you must ask the universe for it. If you want to become a millionaire or a billionaire, ask for it. Since we were kids, we were told that there is a power that lives up in the sky who is listening to us. If we want anything in life, all we need to do is ask through prayer and in time we get it.

Whether you are a spiritual person or not, know this—there is some truth in it. You do not know if you are asking God or the universe but when you ask, you get it. However, there is a small difference between a prayer and asking the universe. In prayer, we just ask without taking responsibility. It is as if we are asking on a whim. But when we use the universe with the belief in connections that exist, we ask with responsibility.

We do not live in a fantasy, but we seek what we deserve. We ask because we believe that we are working hard enough to receive it. We are asking not for results but for things that we must attract in order to get the results.

Do not talk like a kid nagging for a toy with no purpose or ambition. Ask with power and with the feeling that you have the right to receive it, and you deserve it because you have the right intent.

You are not just asking for the results you want, but you are also telling the world what you are willing to do and become to get those results. And the best way to do that is by using affirmations.

Affirmations help you not just ask the universe for things you want but also find the core within yourself. Affirmations are the positive statements you make to yourself with belief and trust in yourself that these statements are true. Actually, those will be the statements you would want to be true about yourself and your life. By making them flow to your subconscious mind by repeating them again and again, you make your mind start believing that they are actually true. And that is when the forces of the universe start to act with the energy radiated by your powerful subconscious mind, and you begin attracting things that actually make the statements true.

Here are a few affirmations you can use in your journey as you transition from job to business:

Manifesting Financial Abundance

I earn abundant income.

I earn more passive income to pay for my desired lifestyle.

I set up my automation tools and systems to work instead of me.

I get paid based on the outcomes and the value I provide.

I enjoy earning money while I sleep, play or am on vacation.

I work less, I earn more.

Excellent income opportunities always appear before me.

I utilize all the time and money I have to create my abundance.

I am living a financially-free lifestyle.

I work as a choice, not by compulsion.

I choose to create abundance with ease, grace, simplicity and freedom.

Winning the 'Mind' Game

I create my life and all my experiences.

I create my financial success.

I play my money game to create a win-win situation.

I am intent on creating wealth and abundance for myself and my clients.

I am inspired and learn from rich and successful people.

I know that money is important, gives freedom and makes life more enjoyable.

I am getting richer doing what I love.

I deserve to charge premium fees because I add value to other people's lives.

I am a great giver and an awesome receiver.

I am genuinely grateful to my lord for everything I possess.

Amazing opportunities always come my way.

My ability to earn, hold and grow my income is expanding daily.

Secrets of the Billionaire Mind

My inner world creates my outer world.

I observe my thoughts and entertain only those that empower me.

I release my non-supportive money experiences from the past.

I create a new and rich future.

I create the exact level of my financial success.

My goal is to become a *crorepati* and more.

I think 'big'.

I choose to help thousands and thousands of people.

I promote my value among others with passion and enthusiasm.

I am an excellent receiver.

I am open and willing to receive massive amounts of money into my life.

I am committed to constantly learn and grow.

Key Takeaways

- When the environment is foggy, things don't look clear and the same is true with your mind. When you have a fog in your head, you can't think straight.

- One way to clear your fog is to use the universal vibrations that create connections between all that exists in the world. And your energies will start flowing in the direction required.
- You meet so many people in life and sometimes you feel like you can trust a person after the first meeting. This happens because your frequency matches with that person's.
- You need to find the people who match your frequency to create possibilities in life, but for that to happen, you must know what your frequency is.
- Tell the universe what you truly want with conviction and the universe will start giving you the right things.

Free Resources

https://app.startupsecrets.in/ch9

Chapter 10

The Final Round

Before you jump into the world of entrepreneurship, you must know that the life of an entrepreneur is different from the life of an employee. Do you know how it is different?

A job needs the right skills, a business needs the right mindset.

A job needs you to manage stress, a business needs you to manage uncertainties.

A job requires you to follow procedures, a business needs you to innovate, experiment.

A job needs you to adapt with technology, a business needs you to adapt with the market.

A job needs you to stay afloat, a business needs you to be a racer.

A job would give you a way to create a safe space, the business provides you the way to create an innovation space.

A job needs you to work with systems, a business needs you to work with people.

An employee needs to meet monthly targets, an entrepreneur needs to achieve daily targets.

An employee is guided by the boss in decisions, an entrepreneur is guided by one's own capacity of understanding.

An employee walks in the direction planned by the company, an entrepreneur makes the company walk in the direction planned by himself or herself.

An employee's life is the life of a follower, an entrepreneur's life is the life of a creator.

An employee has to work within the limits of protocols and policies, an entrepreneur needs to free flow between aspiration and innovation.

An employee answers questions, an entrepreneur questions the answers.

So, let us summarize the questions that the entrepreneur in you needs to ask:

1. Am I happy?
2. Why does my family deserve my time?
3. Am I okay being tame?
4. What is my purpose?
5. Do I believe in myself?

You have already thought about the questions listed above while reading the previous chapters. Now, take a deep breath and take a large sheet of paper and write the answers to the questions. If you have already explored the answers, this should be easy. If not, this is the time to do it.

When you are answering the first question, don't just say yes or no but state all the reasons that make you unhappy with your current life and job.

When you are answering if your family deserves your time, do not just write yes or no but write why they deserve it. If you will give them time, indicate what you hope to be doing with the time spent.

_____

_____

_____

_____

_____

When you are answering the question, 'Am I okay being tame?', do not just write yes or no. Write how you feel when you realize that you are like a tame lion, and if there is something asking you to get out, then write about that feeling too. Say what exactly upsets you and what you want to do about it.

_____

_____

_____

_____

_____

Your purpose statement must be clear as glass with no blotches. This will become the reason you will be taking the path to entrepreneurship.

_____

_____

_____

_____

_____

When answering if you believe in yourself, do not just write yes or no but indicate what reasons make you believe that you can do it or the reasons you cannot do it.

_____

_____

_____

_____

This is just the beginning . . .

Now that you know your purpose, it is time for you to act on it. When you go on any journey, you pack a travel kit in which you keep all the essentials that you will need to complete your journey smoothly and successfully. On the path of entrepreneurship also, you need to take a kit and have everything packed in it so that when you walk the path, you won't have to ever look back.

The first thing you need to pack is the purpose-driven mindset. Your purpose must be clear and personal. It must shape your decisions and actions to an extent that you would not want to compromise with your dream in any way.

The purpose that you have written on your sheet must be kept in a place where you can read it every single day. As you keep reading it, it will get ingrained as your source of inspiration and will guide you. Do this today! You do not have to wait for a business plan to take shape in your head. Just write your purpose, your 'why', and keep it where you can see it every day. Perhaps you can paste it on the wall with 'PURPOSE' written in bold and big letters so you can read it every morning after getting up and every night before you go to bed.

The second thing you need to pack is a plan of action. Dreams can inspire you and purpose can guide you, but without action, your dreams cannot be achieved. So, it is time you had a concrete action plan for your business to take shape. Right now, you do not need to make a plan about how to launch a product, how to market yourself, or how to get finance, but you have to only plan on how to make yourself ready for a business.

What actions should you take to make yourself mentally ready?

Learn: Learn everything about your area of business so you understand it well. You can educate yourself through books, websites, courses, online videos and talking to people in the target industry. Of course, having someone by your side, helping you every step of the way with a proven pathway can certainly help you accelerate at 10X the speed. At this point, be prudent to ensure that your mentor is someone with an ultimate results system who guides you not just in creating a plan but also in creating a mindset that is needed. This can be a big help.

Connect: Connect with the right people who will create an environment for you to keep the right energies flowing. So, to become an entrepreneur, you have to start hanging out with entrepreneurs. That way, you will be able to see how they think, how they make things possible, how they strive in their business, how they innovate and how they become successful. They cannot just be your friends but also your inspiration and guides. Talking to people who will actually understand the passion you have is very important. Your family, friends and colleagues may advise you to play safe and remain in the comfort zone. But other entrepreneurs, whether personally connected to you or not, will not do so. In fact, they will be more than happy to help you understand the stakes and find ways for you to make a grand entry.

In the corporate world, you launch yourself in a race where you are competing with everyone around you. But when you take the path of entrepreneurship, you will realize that you do not have to fight but you will be absorbed as part of the community and will be provided with help and guidance. The world of entrepreneurs is very different from the corporate world. In the corporate world, most people live with a crab mentality, where to rise above, often people tend to pull down others. However, in the world of business, you do not pull down but you transfer energies and inspiration to grow together as a community. There are partnerships made to create growth together. A mutual respect is what prevails in the world of entrepreneurship because everyone is here to learn, thrive, grow and create possibilities. There is no politics that you have to frown upon here. There is no pulling you down by others. And there are no limitations to hold you back.

Purpose: Make your purpose mean more by promising yourself to not rest till your dream is realized. Your purpose needs to be big enough, inspirational enough, important enough and visible enough. It must guide your action plan ahead. You must analyse like a detective and understand it so well that you will never forget it.

Goals: Make a list of goals for your coming five years, then narrow them down further to write your goals for three years to make the five-year ambition possible. After you know what your three years will hold, create an action plan for the first year, and then three months. Suppose your five-year dream is to create a billion-dollar business by launching a mobile app that does good to a million users, your goal for the five-year span would be to build an app and take it to a million users. If you want a million users in five years, how many users should you have in three years? How many in one year? How many in three months? Divide every goal on a timeline that narrows down to three months, and then you will have smaller goals that would look more achievable, and planning your journey will become easy.

What practical actions should you take to make yourself ready?

Bank balance: What is the balance you need in your bank account to keep going if you suddenly quit your job? Have a backup for at least a year that you can use to survive while you are still experimenting with your new business.

Resources: What resources does your business require? In terms of systems, skills, legalities and assets? Write everything down that you will need to have with you if your business is to succeed. This list will depend on your business idea. Suppose you want to create an e-learning system for students, your resources could be an e-learning app, course content such as videos and study material, a database of students, a payment gateway for purchases, a landing page for marketing and so on. If you do not have resources right now, think of a possibility of generating them in the near future. If you have a plan to get resources in the next three months and then use them to create possibilities, you are ready to dive in.

Family buy-in: When you start on your great journey, you will be released from the clutches of the crabs in your office. But if you do not make your family understand how important this is for you, the clutches would not be gone totally because without the buy-in of your family, you could be struggling every day to stay afloat. However, it is not always possible that your family will be supportive. At times, they just do not believe in your ambition and do not find your reasons for leaving a job important enough. In such a scenario, have patience till you show them the results. Ask them to give you time to prove yourself and then, ask them to also promise support if you succeed. This way, both you and your family will be free of questions and apprehensions as time will decide how well you will do and convince them. Remember, with the family it's love, not logic, that prevails. So, you have to play on the trust factor and ask them to support you emotionally.

Remember to do that at the start itself because after you have already started, things can get tough. At the start, you may not be working as per their expectations and could be dwelling more on your business idea than they have the tolerance for. And then things will become tough, not because your business front is in trouble but because you are personally not in the right frame of mind because of the lack of support from your family.

The Plan: You have a purpose and you have goals for the next three months. You also know what resources you need to acquire if you do not have them. You also know that you have to gain the support of your family. So, now is the time to create your plan of action. In this action plan, have slots not just for your business idea but also for your mindset preparation, learning, networking, family, personal growth and resource creation. So, what could you be doing in the next three months?

1. Talk to your family to get their buy-in on the business idea.
2. Book a web domain and create your first website on your own. (It's as simple as making an MS PowerPoint presentation.) Look for the Free Resources section to check the links.
3. Buy a nice notebook and start taking notes on entrepreneurship to use them in practice.

4. Define your product or service clearly and include features, benefits, target and price for each.
5. Talk to 100 prospects who could become your potential clients.

The points listed above are just presented as examples. Your action plan will have different points depending on your business, financial condition and home environment. Against every action item, you must also write specific dates by when you should take certain steps and also a note on how to execute these specific steps.

Now you have everything you require in your travel kit, and you are ready to dive in!

When you are ready as an entrepreneur, you can then make your business idea ready, too, by creating a business plan and marketing plan. Your preparedness as an entrepreneur will help you create the right energies to execute this plan.

All the best for your future! Please do write to me and share your story.

Free Resources

https://app.startupsecrets.in/ch10

Epilogue

I have worked with hundreds of aspiring and existing start-up entrepreneurs and businessmen, and consulted with many organizations over the last few years of my business life. I have learnt from my own journey and from the numerous interactions I had with these entrepreneurs that business is a spiritual journey of an entrepreneur and is beyond the visible logical steps. It is more the journey of a heart that believes in something that's really important to the entrepreneur. And alongside having the heart of a believer, it's highly important that purposeful, meaningful action is what makes things that are believed achievable. Further, the right mindset strengthens both the belief and the capability to take action.

In this book if you explored its depth with me, you would have discovered the exact triggers that I got from my life experiences and interactions with great minds. The next step is obviously taking action so you can apply the lessons learnt and see for yourself how they work.

There are many self-help books written on business and entrepreneurship, and some of them have real power to change your life. But whether the change really happens or not is only revealed after the application of what was learnt. There could be two kinds of readers of these books:

1. People who read and find the knowledge interesting and inspiring but **do not** take action. They have no courage to act.
2. People who are action-takers and would jump at the first technique given in a book to try that in life.

You could be either one of them. If you are an action-taker, well, I am glad for you as you would have already read the book and also applied its lessons since you have reached this page.

However, if you are the former type of reader who could still not gather the courage to take the required step, you might need a bigger push. Do not worry, for most people need a push, some less and some more. If you need a bigger push, I would suggest you use the free resources session where you can interact with me in a live session, and allow me to be your coach for a while. I will help you discover the ways you can start getting immediate results in your life and identifying and removing the anchors that are still holding you back, and how you can take the journey you really want to take.

I am completing this book with the belief that if you are reading these lines, it's for a reason. And the reason is that the universe wants you to move forward and transcend paradigms. Whether you are an existing entrepreneur wanting to grow, or an aspiring entrepreneur stuck in a job trap wanting to launch a start-up of your own, I want you to know that you have a gift that you may want to share with the world. Please feel free to flip through the pages of this book again for a quick revision, and you might find what you are looking for to get ahead in life. If you wish to get more help, all you need to do is simply check out links for some free resources at the start of this book and at the end of each chapter that I am specially creating for the readers of this book.

While these resources come to you absolutely free, I want you to know that people invest lakhs of rupees to get these. So, participate and learn from them as if you are investing a few lakhs to benefit from these resources and get the most amazing results in your business and life.

Super Start-up Success,

Neeraj Kapoor

Free Resources:

With an intention to enable you to generate exponential results in your life and business.

Here is a list of free resources including on-demand courses, live programmes, inspiring downloads and a host of start-up-enabling solutions:

https://app.startupsecrets.in/resources

Acknowledgements

An august group of masters deserve and have my appreciation for their contribution in making this book possible.

I am indebted to my mother, Smt. Bina Kapoor, who inspired me with leadership stories from her experience of leading the women's empowerment movement in her little village, Khachrod, in Madhya Pradesh over fifty-five years ago. In spite of all odds and social taboos, she not only completed her graduation, but also chose to break the barriers by becoming a contributing member of society and serving as a teacher in a government school. Her tenacity, determination, strategic vision, willingness to always strive for the best and make a big difference in the lives of people around, became part of my DNA almost unknowingly. (I probably got these qualities from her in the womb itself.)

I am thankful to my father, Shri Shiam Narain Kapoor, who ingrained in me the core values of courage, commitment, love, giving/forgiving, service before self, success, altruistic contribution and nation-building. He nurtured me to celebrate every moment of life no matter what comes in the way, while he served in the Indian armed forces as a humble foreman at an army base workshop in Agra.

I feel blessed to have Vandana as my wife, who stood by me like a rock in every decision I took. Her sweet smile put me on track whenever I needed it most. Her ability to ask the right questions often helped me to separate the wheat from the chaff.

I thank Gaurang and Vedita, my two teenage angels, who observed and learnt every nuance while I went through the rollercoaster ride of being a start-up entrepreneur and found my way on to the business highway. They are already showing signs of being great leaders in the making. I also would like to thank Meghana Dutta, Pooja Dubey and Tanmay Dubey for their numerous inputs and multiple edits, back and forth while writing this book.

I am also indebted to my gurus, mentors, coaches and teachers, including Brajamohan Das, Anthony Robbins, Werner Erhard, T. Harv Eker, and friends who stood by me in my moments of need and empowered me with the right frame of reference. This helped me take effective action, which resulted in miraculous outcomes on an ongoing basis.

Truly, without each of them giving a part of their life to this book, you wouldn't be benefiting from this work.